The Aztecs
End of a Civilization

Titles in the History's Great Defeats series include:

The Aztecs: End of a Civilization
The British Empire: The End of Colonialism
The Cold War: Collapse of Communism
The Third Reich: Demise of the Nazi Dream

The Aztecs
End of a Civilization

by Joan D. Barghusen

Lucent Books, San Diego, CA

No part of this book may be reproduced or used in any form or by any means, electrical, mechanical, or otherwise, including, but not limited to, photocopy, recording, or any information storage and retrieval system, without prior written permission from the publisher.

Library of Congress Cataloging-in-Publication Data

Barghusen, Joan D., 1935–
    The Aztecs : end of a civilization / by Joan Barghusen.
      p.   cm. — (History's great defeats)
    Includes bibliographical references and index.
    Summary: Discusses the end of the Aztec civilization, including the fragile network of their empire, the arrival of the conquistadors, the Spanish advantages in the areas of weaponry and leadership, the role of Montezuma, and the aftermath of the conflict.
    ISBN 1-56006-620-2 (lib. : alk. paper)
    1. Aztecs—Juvenile literature. 2. Mexico—History—Conquest, 1519–1540—Juvenile literature. [1. Aztecs. 2. Indians of Mexico. 3. Mexico—History—Conquest, 1519–1540.] I. Title. II. Series.

F1219.73 .B357   2000
972'.02—dc21
                                                            99-046849

Table of Contents

Foreword

HISTORY IS FILLED with tales of dramatic encounters that sealed the fates of empires or civilizations, changing them or causing them to disappear forever. One of the best known events began in 334 B.C., when Alexander, king of Macedonia, led his small but formidable Greek army into Asia. In the short span of only ten years, he brought Persia, the largest empire the world had yet seen, to its knees, earning him the nickname forever after associated with his name—"the Great." The demise of Persia, which at its height stretched from the shores of the Mediterranean Sea in the west to the borders of India in the east, was one of history's most stunning defeats. It occurred primarily because of some fatal flaws in the Persian military system, disadvantages the Greeks had exploited before, though never as spectacularly as they did under Alexander.

First, though the Persians had managed to conquer many peoples and bring huge territories under their control, they had failed to create an individual fighting man who could compare with the Greek hoplite. A heavily armored infantry soldier, the hoplite fought in a highly effective and lethal battlefield formation—the phalanx. Possessed of better armor, weapons, and training than the Persians, Alexander's soldiers repeatedly crushed their Persian opponents. Second, the Persians for the most part lacked generals of the caliber of their Greek counterparts. And when Alexander invaded, Persia had the added and decisive disadvantage of facing one of the greatest generals of all time. When the Persians were defeated, their great empire was lost forever.

Other world powers and civilizations have fallen in a like manner. They have succumbed to some combination of inherent fatal flaws or

6

disadvantages, to political and/or military mistakes, and even to the personal failings of their leaders.

Another of history's great defeats was the sad demise of the North American Indian tribes at the hands of encroaching European civilization from the sixteenth to nineteenth centuries. In this case, all of the tribes suffered from the same crippling disadvantages. Among the worst, they lacked the great numbers, the unity, and the advanced industrial and military hardware possessed by the Europeans. Still another example, one closer to our own time, was the resounding defeat of Nazi Germany by the Allies in 1945, which brought World War II, the most disastrous conflict in history, to a close. Nazi Germany collapsed for many reasons. But one of the most telling was that its leader, Adolf Hitler, sorely underestimated the material resources and human resolve of the Allies, especially the United States. In the end, Germany was in a very real sense submerged by a massive and seemingly relentless tidal wave of Allied bombs, tanks, ships, and soldiers.

Seen in retrospect, a good many of the fatal flaws, drawbacks, and mistakes that caused these and other great defeats from the pages of history seem obvious. It is only natural to wonder why, in each case, the losers did not realize their limitations and/or errors sooner and attempt to avert disaster. But closer examination of the events, social and political trends, and leading personalities involved usually reveals that complex factors were at play. Arrogance, fear, ignorance, stubbornness, innocence, and other attitudes held by nations, peoples, and individuals often colored and shaped their reactions, goals, and strategies. And it is both fascinating and instructive to reconstruct how such attitudes, as well as the fatal flaws and mistakes themselves, contributed to the losers' ultimate demise.

Each volume in Lucent Books' *History's Great Defeats* series is designed to provide the reader with diverse learning tools for exploring the topic at hand. Each well-informed, clearly written text is supported and enlivened by substantial quotes by the actual people involved, as well as by later historians and other experts; and these primary and secondary sources are carefully documented. Each volume also supplies the reader with an extensive Works Consulted list, guiding him or her to further research on the topic. These and other research tools, including glossaries and time lines, afford the reader a thorough understanding of how and why one of history's most decisive defeats occurred and how these events shaped our world.

Spanish Adventurers and the Land
of Montezuma

IN THE EARLY PART of the sixteenth century, Spaniard Hernán Cortés, searching for gold, led a small band of European adventurers into the Valley of Mexico. The Spanish invaders hoped to discover the source of Mexican gold from the Aztec ruler Montezuma when they reached him in his capital city of Tenochtitlán. What Cortés and his men found as they approached Tenochtitlán astounded them, for Montezuma's capital was the great urban center of a complex civilization as yet unknown to Europeans.

Is This a Dream?

Tenochtitlán was built on an island in the southern part of a large lake. High causeways made of earth and stone extended to the south, west, and north, connecting the capital to towns and cities on the mainland. As the Spaniards entered the capital city along the great southern causeway, foot soldier Bernal Díaz del Castillo, a member of the Spanish expedition, took note of the soldiers' reactions:

> When we saw so many cities and villages built both in the water and on dry land, and this straight, level causeway, we couldn't restrain our admiration. It was like the enchantments told about in the book of Amadis [*Amadis deGaula*, a popular novel of the time], because of the high towers, *cúes* [temples], and other buildings, all of masonry, which rose from the water. Some of our soldiers asked if what we saw was not a dream. It is not to be wondered at that I write it

8

down here in this way, for there is much to ponder over that I do not know how to describe, since we were seeing things that had never before been heard of, or seen, or even dreamed about.[1]

In the city itself were wide streets and canals, laid out in orderly fashion and leading to great open plazas with many-roomed palaces and beautiful gardens. In the plazas stood tall, stepped pyramid towers with temples at the top for the Aztec gods. The Spaniards visited the city's main market and marveled at the products and goods too numerous to describe, all arranged in systematic fashion. Bernal Díaz reports, "There were soldiers among us who had been in many parts of the world, in Constantinople and Rome and all over Italy, who said that they had never before seen a market place so large and so well laid out, and so filled with people."[2]

How Should Montezuma Respond?

The throngs of people, with their wealth of products that amazed the Spaniards, were members of the last of several civilizations that rose and fell in Mexico over a period of two thousand years. At their head was the Aztec emperor Montezuma. Although he was the unchallenged leader of the largest empire in Mesoamerica, Montezuma did not know how to deal with the armed strangers who insisted on coming to see him, even though he had sent them many gifts of the gold

Hernán Cortés and his soldiers marveled at the sight of the magnificent city of Tenochtitlán.

Montezuma's failure to act quickly in defending his empire from the Spanish invaders may have contributed to the empire's defeat.

they sought. The native leader found the reports of Cortés and his men as incredible as the Spaniards found his city. The strangers on their way to see him were said to be different in appearance from the people he knew, and the ships in which they had arrived were so large that they appeared to be mountains floating in the sea. How the emperor should respond to these mysterious people was not clear, for nothing in his own experience or in the traditions handed down by his ancestors had prepared him for this meeting.

The Fall of the Aztecs and Old Mexico

The outcome of the encounter between the Aztecs and the invaders of Mexico is well known. It has been almost five hundred years since Montezuma's empire fell to the Spanish conquistadors, aided by natives of Mexico eager to throw off the dominance of their Aztec overlords. Seeing only an opportunity to free themselves of Aztec control, the natives who supported Cortés did not foresee the monumental changes that the Spanish conquest would bring.

The victory that laid waste the capital city of the Aztec empire opened the door to Spanish control of all of Mexico and part of Central America. Within a few years of the conquest, Spanish settlers were bringing their own culture to the land they called New Spain, changing forever the native way of life. The conquered Indians were powerless to resist the changes imposed on their society. The Spanish brought a new religion, installed a new government and economy, and even brought the crops and animals of Europe to be tended in Spain's new province. Required to pay tribute to the Spanish overlords, the natives became second-class citizens in the new order in their homeland.

From the Aztec point of view, the Spanish conquest of Mexico was a disaster. From Cortés's point of view, it was a grand achievement by bold fighters who overcame all odds to win land and wealth for themselves and their king. Later observers have had questions as well as opinions.

Why Did the Aztecs Lose?

Why the Aztecs lost has puzzled historians and military scholars for centuries. The Spaniards were few in number, whereas the Aztecs were known to mount armies with hundreds of thousands of warriors. On the face of it, Montezuma should have been able to dispatch the conquistadors with no problem. But he did not. Neither did the two emperors who followed him.

History does not provide all the answers to the questions raised by the events of those months between April 1519 and August 1521 when the Spanish and Aztecs met, negotiated, clashed, and finally fought. But there is no disagreement on the ending: The capital city that the Aztecs built, and the Spaniards admired, was destroyed, and so was the empire it represented. How and why the Aztecs fell to the Spanish, and the earth-shaking consequences of that defeat for the indigenous peoples of Mexico, is a fascinating and important story to know.

The Conquistadors and Their Mission

Chapter 1

IN FEBRUARY 1519, a few hundred soldiers, led by thirty-four-year-old Hernán Cortés, set sail from the Spanish province of Cuba bound for the eastern coast of what is now Mexico. Theirs was the third expedition sent by Diego Velázquez, the governor of Cuba, to explore the rich lands to the west, where the natives were said to wear ornaments of gold.

Cortés's official mission was to look for members of Juan de Grijalva's expedition, which had sailed in 1518 and had not yet returned, and for other Spaniards who might have been lost on the Yucatán peninsula during previous explorations. In addition, Cortés was authorized to explore, trade, and learn the source of gold. He was to treat the natives well and instruct them in the basics of Christianity, for it was known that the natives worshiped idols and practiced human sacrifice. And at each place he landed he was to read to the natives the *requerimiento*, the legal document by which Spain laid claim to new territories, so that they would know they were under the rule of King Charles.

Governor Velázquez had not authorized Cortés to begin a war of conquest or to establish settlements. Indeed, the governor expected to settle the new lands himself and was waiting for permission from King Charles of Spain.

Cortés Takes Charge

Cortés, however, appears to have had different ideas about his part in the expedition from the outset. One of the soldiers who accompanied him, Bernal Díaz del Castillo, wrote in his memoirs of the conquest that Cortés made sweeping promises to those who would join his ex-

The Spanish in the West Indies

Hernán Cortés reached Mexico more than twenty-five years after
Columbus had landed in the Bahama Islands, part of an archipelago that
stretches from the southern tip of Florida to the northeast coast of
South America. The Europeans' discovery of these islands, called the Indies because they were thought to be near India, set off a stream of voy-
ages bringing Spanish colonists and conquistadors to the New World.

In 1493 more than one thousand Spanish settlers arrived in Hispaniola, the large island of present-day Haiti and the Dominican Repub-
lic. By 1509 Spaniards had captured the islands of Puerto Rico and
Jamaica. In 1511 they took over Cuba. By 1513 they had established
a settlement far to the south in present-day Panama, believing this
narrow strip of the mainland to be another island.

The Spaniards came to the west expecting to find gold or become
wealthy landowners. But as a result of changes they brought and their
harsh treatment of the natives, most of the islands' local population
soon died. Without native workers for the mines and fields, the islands were not productive, and the Spanish continued their search for
rich, new lands.

When Cortés's expedition left Cuba for outlying lands, said to be a
week's sail to the west, Europeans did not yet know that the conti-
nents of North and South America existed. The Spaniards expected
to find only more islands.

pedition. "To the sound of drums and trumpets he had proclaimed in
the name of His Majesty, in the name of Diego Velázquez as royal
governor, and in his own name as his captain general that whoever
might wish to go in his company should receive his share of the
riches that might be captured and a grant of lands and Indians after
the country was pacified."[3]

According to Díaz, Cortés's expedition of eleven ships carried
508 soldiers, mostly Spaniards. Of these, he says, some were gentle-
men and a few were knights. Many of the Spanish members were
men in their twenties, often younger sons in families of the lesser nobility. These young men, whose older brothers would inherit their fathers' lands and money, sought fortunes along with adventure in the
New World. Their bold and effective fighting would earn them the
name of conquistadors, or "conquerors."

Some of the soldiers were seasoned fighters; a few, like Díaz,
had been on one or both of the earlier expeditions and had already

Cortés's fleet sails toward the rich lands of Mexico. The official mission wasn't to claim new territories but to search for a previous expedition that was lost.

experienced warfare with the natives. Some had special skills and served not only as fighting men but also as blacksmiths, carpenters, or experts at repairing weapons. Several expedition members were educated men who had served as officials in government or business. One was a doctor and two were priests. Díaz says the soldiers included thirty-two crossbowmen and thirteen musketeers, and among the weapons were some ship's guns, four small cannon, and a large quantity of powder and balls for the firearms. The conquistadors brought sixteen horses—only a few because the animals were expensive and difficult to transport—as well as war dogs, which were commonly used in European warfare of the time.

At some point during the preparations for departure, Velázquez began to distrust Cortés's motivations and tried to prevent the ships from embarking. But Cortés, confident, ambitious, and adventuresome, was determined to go. Evading the governor, he lifted anchor and made a hasty departure. Far from discouraging Cortés, the withdrawal of Velázquez's support had had an opposite effect. It intensified his will to succeed because Cortés knew that success was his best hope of deflecting punishment for defying the governor's wishes.

Who Was Cortés?

Captain general Hernán Cortés had never led a military expedition before. He was a Spaniard who had come to Spain's island outposts in the West Indies as a young man, hoping to make a fortune mining gold. After a dozen years in various military and administrative positions, he had become close to Diego Velázquez. According to researcher Hugh

Hernán Cortés

Hernán Cortés was born about 1484 in the town of Medellín in Extremadura, a district of Castile in Spain. With a history of armed conflict among powerful families, Extremadura produced many men of action who became conquistadors in the Americas. Cortés's father, a minor nobleman with no title and little money, also served as a soldier, and Cortés grew up in a world in which the skills of horsemanship and military arts were commonplace.

An only child, Cortés was educated in the Catholic church. He served as an altar boy in his youth and remained a pious Catholic throughout his life. He heard mass or prayers regularly, even on march, and he carried to the conquest of Mexico the mission of converting the natives to Christianity.

When he was about twelve years old, Cortés lived with his mother's relatives in Salamanca. Presumably he attended classes at the university there, for he learned some Latin and became familiar with both law and classic literature. Later he spent time in Seville and Valladolid, cities where he had the opportunity to observe life at Spain's royal court.

A desire for wealth drove the ambitious Cortés to command the expedition that would eventually conquer Mexico.

Some who knew him as a young man said that Cortés liked to read but that he liked to gamble and to fight even more. He traveled and worked in several Spanish cities, probably serving as a notary, an official familiar with the law. But soon Cortés began to look to faraway places for the active life he craved and a chance to make his name and fortune. At age twenty-two, he joined an expedition to the West Indies, the farthest outpost of Spanish civilization. Known to be ambitious, clever, daring, and cool under pressure, he rose in the ranks of officials and was a magistrate in Santiago, Cuba, when he was chosen to lead the expedition that would conquer Mexico.

Thomas, Cortés "probably accompanied Velázquez in his first drive through Cuba, in search of places in which to found towns. He is said to have had built the first foundry and the first hospital in Cuba. He must afterwards have seen the reports, *relaciones*, which Velázquez sent to the King about his achievements. Probably he helped to draft them."[4] These tasks were all preludes to activities he would later perform in the conquest of Mexico.

Governor Velázquez had learned to respect Cortés's ability as a leader. Thomas continues, "Hernán Cortés in 1518 was known to be resourceful, capable, and good with words, in both speech and writing. He talked well: always having the right expression for the occasion, and agreeable in conversation. In his way he was already experienced in politics."[5] Cortés's talent for diplomatic speech would play an important role in dealing with both Spaniards and natives, but his words would have to be translated for the non-Spanish-speaking Indians.

Cortés Among the Mayans

Cortés had brought two Mayan Indians, prisoners from an earlier expedition, to serve as interpreters. But their knowledge of Spanish was limited. A fortunate discovery soon brought Cortés a better interpreter. On the Yucatán coast, he located and ransomed from his Indian captor a Spaniard named Gerónimo de Aguilar. Marooned by a shipwreck, Aguilar had lived for several years as a slave among the Yucatán Indians and spoke their Mayan language. With his ability to translate Mayan into Spanish, Aguilar made it possible for Cortés to communicate more fully with the natives of the peninsula.

When the conquistadors met the Indians in battle for the first time at Potonchan in the Mayan province of Tabasco (the present state of Tabasco in southern Mexico), they found themselves greatly outnumbered. They managed to drive off the Indians only when soldiers on horseback arrived to reinforce the Spanish foot soldiers. Never having seen horses before, the terrified natives were quickly routed. This experience taught the Spanish that even a small force of cavalry could break up the Indians' fighting formations.

Ross Hassig, a historian of Aztec warfare, states that the Spanish changed their battle tactics in response to experiences with the Mayan Indians: "They learned that minimal combat units of around two hundred men were necessary to resist massive Indian attacks, that harquebuses and crossbows were effective against Indian armour, that artillery was extremely disruptive and, finally, that mounted lancers could disrupt formations and force the Indians to flee."[6] Although Cortés soon left the lands of the Mayan behind, in fighting them he had gained an understanding of Indian warfare that helped prepare him for future encounters with the Aztecs of central Mexico.

Marina Joins the Expedition

In making peace, the Mayans of Tabasco gave the conquistadors gifts, including a number of women. One was a young Aztec woman who had been a slave among the Mayans for several years. This remarkable young woman became known as Malinche, or Marina, as she was called after she was baptized as a Christian. Like Aguilar, Marina spoke Mayan, but she also spoke Nahuatl, the language of the Aztecs. As the expedition moved north into the land of Nahuatl speakers, Marina interpreted the Nahuatl into Mayan for Aguilar, who then translated it into Spanish for Cortés. Before long Marina learned Spanish, too, and was able to translate directly for Cortés. Raised in a noble family before she was enslaved, Marina was thoroughly familiar with the Aztec empire and its customs. She became Cortés's trusted adviser and remained at his side throughout the conquest. Both Spanish and native sources agree that her aid in the conquest was invaluable and that her loyalty to Cortés never failed.

Cortés in Search of Gold

Gold was the spur that motivated Cortés and the lure he offered the men who followed him. But besides gold, Cortés was driven by a desire for the honor and fame that would come from winning lands for Spain and converting souls to the Catholic faith. At every meeting with natives, Cortés told them about his religion. He asked them to give up worshiping their idols and making human sacrifices and to become Christians. He also told them that he served a great king, Charles of Spain, who had sent him to them in peace.

Cortés hoped that winning the rich lands of Mexico for the king would bring him royal patronage and protect him from the wrath of the governor he had angered. The Indians told him gold came from

Marina

One of the most important members of Cortés's expedition joined the group in the Yucatán. She was a gift from the Mayan Indians of Tabasco. Eighteen years old at the time, the young Indian woman's name was Malinali, a word meaning "grass" in her native tongue.

Malinali was the daughter of two native rulers. Both her mother and father were heads of small villages in an area just south of the lands controlled by Montezuma. As the only child, she would have inherited the positions of both parents. But her father died when she was young, and after her mother remarried, a boy was born into the family. Perhaps so her new son would inherit the chiefdom, Malinali's mother sold her daughter, then eight to ten years old, to Mexican traders, who then sold her to the Mayas. Malinali had been a slave for at least eight years before the Mayas gave her to Cortés.

The young slave girl had learned to speak the Mayan language of the land to which she had been taken, but she also retained the Nahuatl language spoken in her original home. With her knowledge of these two languages and a flair for learning Spanish, Malinali soon became indispensable as Cortés's main interpreter and principal adviser in dealing with the natives.

Marina's interpreting skills were invaluable to the success of Cortés's mission.

The young interpreter was often referred to as Malinche, but the Spanish called her Marina, the name she took when she was baptized into the Christian faith. She was greatly respected by the Spanish for her abilities and her value to their cause. The soldier Bernal Díaz del Castillo wrote that Marina was an "excellent woman," "brave" and "shrewd," "of good appearance, intelligent, and poised."

Mexico, inland to the west, where the great lord Montezuma ruled. As the expedition approached the lands of the Mexica, or Aztecs, Cortés made up his mind to journey inland to the heart of the Aztec empire and locate the source of gold.

Strangers in the Land

Cortés's arrival on the eastern Mexican coast in spring 1519 did not escape the Aztec emperor's attention. The outer reaches of Montezuma's empire were monitored constantly by spies and government officials, as well as by *pochteca*, the important long-distance traders who traveled throughout and even beyond the lands controlled by the Aztecs. A system of runners carried messages, including manuscripts in pictorial writing, to and from the capital at Tenochtitlán. Thus activities in the land were quickly known to the Aztec emperor. Reports of the newcomers reached him within two days' time.

Montezuma's agents on the coast had been keeping a special watch for such strangers for a year because in 1518 an Aztec workman had told of seeing "mountains" afloat in the eastern sea. Upon investigating, Montezuma's trusted advisers had seen strange men with white skin, beards, and long hair fishing from small boats and then returning to the floating "mountains."

Montezuma had then dispatched emissaries to meet these strangers and try to find out more about them. His servants took gifts of food and richly decorated cloaks; in return, the strangers gave them hard biscuits and necklaces of glass beads. The parties feasted together, and before leaving, the strangers promised to return to Mexico soon. The ships' biscuits and beads were taken back to Tenochtitlán, where Montezuma examined them, showed them to officials of his court, and finally offered them to his gods. He ordered his officials to keep a close watch on the coast in case the strangers should return.

Montezuma ordered his spies to report the presence of any intruders on Aztec land.

The strangers who had arrived in 1518 were members of the expedition led by Juan de Grijalva. They were the first Spaniards the Mexica had seen. But stories of strangers had been circulating for years, beginning as early as 1502, the same year that Montezuma became emperor. The tales told of men with white skin and beards who had appeared in the islands to the east. These unsettling stories had troubled Montezuma greatly, and the appearance of Grijalva and his men filled him with dread. These events were completely out of the ordinary, and it was impossible to know what they meant. The emperor looked to his advisers, priests, and magicians to tell him the significance of these happenings, but none of their interpretations satisfied him. Native sources say that he grew ever more apprehensive, fearing that both he and the empire were in grave danger. Montezuma was still searching for answers when messengers announced that bearded strangers had come again.

Cortés Arrives in the Land of the Totonacs

It was April 1519 when Cortés, like Grijalva before him, anchored his ships off the Mexican coast in the land of the Totonacs, near present-day Veracruz. The Totonacs were Aztec vassals, and Montezuma's representative on the coast approached the Spaniards by canoe, demanding to know their business. Cortés replied that he was an ambassador of a great king and wished to talk with Montezuma. The official said he would send this message to the capital; meanwhile, apparently acting on previous orders, he brought food and gifts to the strangers, including workers to build shelters for them. He treated the Spanish with great respect and left two thousand servants at Cortés's disposal. "But among the two thousand were doubtless spies, priests, and sorcerers," says researcher Hugh Thomas. "Presumably these arrangements were made on Montezuma's suggestion. Hospitality was mixed with tactics."[7] Montezuma was on guard.

Among the gifts the official offered were gold ornaments. Cortés then asked the official if the emperor had gold, saying that he needed it to cure a sickness of the heart that some of his men had. The official answered that Montezuma did in fact have gold. As Thomas writes, "That exchange could not have been more dangerous for the Mexica."[8]

To impress Montezuma's men, Cortés had the ships' cannon fired and the horses exercised on the beach. The Mexica were greatly frightened by the noise and force of the firearms and by the speed and power of the horses. Aztec artists made sketches of all they saw for messengers to take to Montezuma. The emperor's representative asked that a helmet being worn by one of the soldiers also be sent to Montezuma, apparently because it resembled a headdress of one of the Aztec gods. Cortés agreed, but cleverly asked that it be returned filled with gold dust.

Montezuma Learns of Cortés

When word of these events reached Montezuma, the Aztec leader was thrown into despair. Without knowing who the strangers were, he could not decide how he should respond to them. Though he had been both priest and warrior, there was nothing in the Aztec traditions to guide him in these unheard-of circumstances.

Montezuma meets with his trusted advisers, some of whom thought the light-skinned, bearded invaders might be gods who had come to destroy Aztec civilization.

To make matters worse, his advisers had no consensus of opin-
ion. Some thought the strangers were simply powerful new enemies
who should be repelled. But others thought that, if they were ambassadors of a great king, as they claimed, they should be shown the respect that Aztecs always afforded diplomats. A more troubling possibility was that the strangers might be lost leaders returning to claim
the land. The Mexica were relative newcomers in central Mexico.
Surrounded by the ruins of great kingdoms that no longer existed,
they knew their own empire, too, could one day fall.

But the worst possibility was that the strangers might be gods
who had come to destroy the established order of Aztec rule. The
Aztecs believed that four worlds—or suns, as they called them—had
existed before them, and each had been destroyed. Their time was the
fifth sun, and they believed it, too, would end in destruction.

Montezuma's Response

Not surprising, Montezuma and his advisers did not want the strangers to
come to Tenochtitlán. The emperor responded by sending a message that
he could not meet with the unexpected visitors; his duties kept him from
leaving Tenochtitlán, and the trip from the coast was too long and dangerous for the strangers to attempt to come to him. At the same time he
sent magnificent gifts of gold, featherwork, embroidered cloth, and jew-
els. Indian sources say that he also secretly sent magicians with orders to
cast spells against the strangers and chase them away.

Montezuma's gifts were probably designed to impress the strangers
with his might as a powerful lord commanding great lands and riches.
"From what we know of Mexica and indeed of Amerindian cultures,"
states historian Inga Clendinnen, "Moctezuma's 'gifts' were statements
of dominance: gestures of wealth and unmatchable liberality made the
more glorious by the extravagant humility of their giving."[9] Cortés, however, probably did not understand the fabulous gifts in this way. Rather,
historians believe, he interpreted them as either gestures of submission
or attempts at bribery. Either way, they did not convince him to abandon
his plan to visit the Aztec capital.

Cortés Prepares to Go to Tenochtitlán

Cortés repeated his request to see Montezuma, saying that his own
king would be displeased if he returned without meeting with the

Language and Writing of the Aztecs

The language spoken by the Aztecs and most other natives of central Mexico was Nahuatl. The Aztecs had not yet developed the skill of writing their speech in alphabetic form. But they made pictorial books that were drawn and painted by artists on native paper made of bark, animal skins, or cloth. These books, like the ones that brought messages to Montezuma about the Spaniards, were then "read" by scribes and record keepers who memorized the stories or information depicted in them.

When the Spaniards wrote names and words in Nahuatl, they used the letters of their own Spanish, or Latin, alphabet to record the sounds they heard. These letters, however, were not always a perfect match for the sounds of Nahuatl. For example, Nahuatl contained the sounds of *p, t,* and *c* but not the related sounds of *b, d,* and *g.* Similarly, there were differences between Nahuatl vowel sounds and vowels in Spanish. Thus, the translation of Nahuatl words and names into Spanish was an approximation of the sounds heard by the person who wrote them down.

For this reason, Aztec words and names are often spelled in differing ways. The spelling *Montezuma* became the early conventional way of writing the Aztec emperor's name. But different forms are common, such as *Moteuczoma* and *Motecuhzoma.* Some are based on more recent language studies that attempt to render a pronunciation that is thought to be closer to the Aztec original.

Aztec emperor in person. Sending more gifts, Montezuma reiterated that Cortés was under no circumstances to come to Tenochtitlán. But Cortés was not to be discouraged. Viewing Montezuma's continued refusal to see him as a sign of weakness, he prepared to march inland in pursuit of his plan to deliver the Aztec lands to Charles of Spain.

Before he left the coast, however, Cortés established a town in the name of Spain, calling it Villa Rica de la Vera Cruz, the "Rich Town of the True Cross," located about forty miles north of present-day Veracruz. He devised a plan for his men to elect him mayor, an act that made him the supreme Spanish power in the new land. He left the town in the care of a small band of soldiers and 150 other men, mostly sailors. Villa Rica would be Cortés's stronghold on the coast and a source for supplies as the conquistadors moved inland.

The Aztec Empire: A Fragile Network

WHEN THE SPANISH LANDED in Montezuma's territory, the Aztecs ruled the largest and mightiest empire in Mesoamerica. Historian Ross Hassig calls the Aztec empire a strong one: "The Aztecs were undoubtedly the greatest power in Mesoamerica and, without external intervention, there was no major threat to the internal security of Tenochtitlan." [10] But the arrival of the Spaniards introduced a new element into the existing balance of power, revealing weaknesses in the empire that would contribute greatly to its downfall.

The Aztec Empire Was a Tributary One

The Aztec empire was a loosely organized network of cities and towns that acknowledged the Aztecs as their overlords. The residents expressed their submission by making payments, called tribute, in the form of goods and services. The empire embraced many different ethnic groups with their own languages and gods, but underlying cultural similarities linked all of Mesoamerica. The basis of wealth was agriculture, with maize and beans as the main crops. Different people worshiped their own particular gods, but many gods were accepted. And the people shared a belief that the gods were nourished by sacrifices of human blood.

In building their empire, the Aztecs had first achieved dominance over their neighbors in and around Lake Texcoco and its four smaller, interconnected lakes, which occupied the southern part of the Valley of Mexico, the area that is today Mexico City. Then they expanded their tributary network outward until their subject towns

Who Are the Aztecs?
Who Are the Mexica?

The term *Aztecs* can be confusing. Sometimes it seems to refer only to the people of Tenochtitlán. And sometimes it refers to a larger range of indigenous people living in central Mexico. Both uses are valid.

The name *Aztec* comes from the word *Aztlan*. Aztlan was the name of the mythical island homeland of a tribe of people who migrated from the north into central Mexico. Along the way they quarreled and split into separate groups. The group that later called themselves the Mexica continued on to the Valley of Mexico, where they lived a sub-servient life among other tribes on the shores of Lake Texcoco. For a while they lived among the Culhua, who were descendants of the Toltecs, an earlier great civilization north of the valley. For this reason they sometimes called themselves the Culhua-Mexica. When forced to leave by the Culhua, the Mexica were instructed by a priest of their god Huitzilopochtli to look for an eagle perched on a cactus as a sign of where they should settle. They found their new home on an island in the lake, and here they began to build Tenochtitlán and to found their empire.

The people who built the city and the empire were the Mexica. When they are referred to as Mexica or Culhua-Mexica, the intention is often to differentiate them from the many other related ethnic groups living in the Valley of Mexico. The term *Aztec* is accepted as a more general term that includes the Mexica but also all the other people of the valley at the time of the conquest. Thus, the Mexica are Aztecs, but not all Aztecs are Mexica.

stretched throughout central Mexico, from the Atlantic Ocean on the east to the Pacific on the west. The empire had advanced in directions where smaller cities and towns could not effectively resist conquest and in directions where coveted resources were to be found. For example, not long before the Spanish arrived, the Aztecs had secured the province of Oaxaca, far beyond the empire's frontiers to the south. This territory was important because it was the source of the green plumes of the quetzal bird that were used in the king's ceremonial dress. Although the Aztecs did not control all the land leading to Oaxaca, they defended a corridor through non-Aztec lands that gave them access to the new province.

By the time Cortés arrived, the Aztecs depended on a far-flung economic network to provide the wealth that sustained their empire. These resources were necessary to keep in place the hierarchy of emperor and

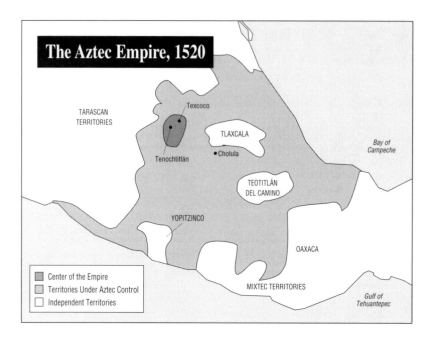

The Aztec Empire, 1520

TARASCAN
TERRITORIES

Texcoco

TLAXCALA

Bay of
Campeche

Tenochtitlán   •Cholula

TEOTITLÁN
DEL CAMINO

YOPITZINCO

OAXACA

Center of the Empire
Territories Under Aztec Control   MIXTEC TERRITORIES
Independent Territories   Gulf of
Tehuantepec

nobles that ruled Aztec society. Much of the tribute was used to provide luxury products for the elite and as gifts the emperor gave to the
favored.

The Aztecs Relied on Force to Dominate

Tributaries were brought under Aztec domination and kept under
control by force or the threat of force. Each year, the Aztecs' powerful army brought new lands into the empire and reclaimed ones that
had rebelled.

The Aztecs were able to persuade some towns to submit without
a fight because, as Ross Hassig points out,

> They also waged campaigns of intimidation against cities
> they did not attack directly. Emissaries were sent to such
> cities to ask that they become subjects of the Aztec king—
> usually on reasonably favorable terms. Both the proximity of
> a large, trained, and obviously successful army and the ob-
> ject lessons burning around them [nearby towns that had
> been torched] led many cities to capitulate peacefully.[11]

Though tributaries were forced to contribute to the Aztecs' empire, there were advantages to being part of the system. Member

towns became part of a vast trading network and were protected from invasions by other hostile people. However, researcher Frederic Hicks notes that it was often not the commoners who benefited the most but the local leaders: "They were dependent on the continued patronage of the imperial rulers, but they were given valuable gifts by these same rulers, they participated with them in lavish feasts, they received lands, and they could count on imperial support as they exploited the common people of their own realms."[12]

The Aztec Army Was a Seasonal One

To enforce his commands, the Aztec emperor relied on a powerful army. However, this body of troops functioned only in the war season of each year, which began in late November after the harvest and continued until the rains began in the spring. Sometime around April, the army disbanded for the agricultural months because the men were needed for farming. Ross Hassig explains:

> Only during the dry period following the harvest were large numbers of men available for such [military] service, when there were adequate food supplies to sustain them en route, and roads were passable and streams fordable by large armies. This is why Aztec wars took place primarily between December and April. During the summer rainy season, most of the commoners were engaged in agricultural and related pursuits and could not be diverted without damage to the economy.[13]

Since all peoples in the region farmed during the same months, the seasonal nature of Montezuma's army did not put the Aztecs at a disadvantage in warfare with other Mesoamerican groups. But it did leave them unprepared for war when the Spanish arrived, for Cortés had landed in Mexico during the agricultural season, and it would be months before Montezuma's army reached full strength.

Shifting Allegiances Make the Empire Unstable

The Aztecs seldom replaced a conquered area's leaders. Because the Aztecs' main interest was in tribute, the goal of conquest was not to destroy an area but to leave it intact to produce wealth. The best way to ensure continued production was to retain the local leadership. Unless the area rebelled or interfered with political interests of the

Tribute Supports the State and Religion

The cities and towns of the Aztec empire paid tribute to Tenochtitlán in goods and services. Since the capital city was located on a small island, it had few resources to support its people and depended on its tributaries for even the most basic supplies, such as food. By the time of the conquest, Tenochtitlán was lavishly supported by contributions from its subjects. Tribute included many and varied manufactured objects, specialty items of an area, labor, and military service. A share of the tribute went to the local leaders responsible for collecting it.

The ceremonial costumes, fine jewelry, and ritual objects of obsidian or greenstone worn by the kings and nobles in elaborate public rituals were acquired as tribute. Their display proclaimed power and wealth. Tribute might also consist of soldiers or porters drafted to carry supplies for the army. Or it might include victims for sacrifice to the gods.

The Aztecs believed it was necessary to perform human sacrifices to appease the gods.

The Aztecs believed it was necessary to feed the gods with the blood and hearts of human sacrifices so that the gods, in turn, would sustain them with the good things in life. As the empire grew rich, more tribute was needed to provide for the growing body of nobles, and thus more sacrifices were needed to satisfy the gods. The Aztecs' ongoing wars of conquest provided for these needs of state and religion.

When the great pyramid of Huitzilopochtli and Tlaloc, Tenochtitlán's main ceremonial center, was renovated in 1487, rulers from all over Mexico were invited to the dedication ceremony. With the wealth of tribute, the emperor entertained his visitors in luxury and watched with them as thousands of captives were sacrificed in testimony to the power of the Mexica and their gods.

empire, the Aztecs relied on the leadership already in place to keep order and collect tribute.

With local leadership intact, areas retained a strong sense of their own identity. Moreover, leaders who had submitted to the Aztecs because of fear or an inability to resist their military power felt little loyalty to the empire. Thus, tributaries often shifted allegiances when they thought another alliance would better serve their interests or if they perceived that the Aztecs had weakened. This tendency to fall away was especially strong in towns far from Tenochtitlán, where people had little connection with the Aztecs, or in recently conquered areas that were not socially integrated into the empire.

Ross Hassig explains how weaknesses in the coalition, or network, of Aztec-dominated cities posed a danger to the empire.

As long as the core of the coalition remained strong, it was in the allied cities' best interests to adhere to it. But because each city retained its own leadership with its own goals and ambitions, the system was unstable. Any weakness in the core alliance reduced its ability to enforce adherence and offered an opportunity for cities to withdraw.[14]

Such cycles of alliance and rupture could occur in rapid succession. For example, not long before the Spanish arrived, the town of Huexotzinco had withdrawn its allegiance from the Aztecs in favor of the independent province of Tlaxcala, the Aztecs' bitterest enemy. The new arrangement did not satisfy the Huexotzincans, however, and they soon renewed their alliance with the Aztecs. The easy transfer of allegiance would become a deadly weakness for the Aztecs when the Spanish invaded their domain and challenged Aztec power.

Totonacs Ally with Cortés

The land of the Totonacs, which Cortés and his men reached in June 1519, was at the eastern edge of the Aztec empire, approximately 250 miles from the capital at Tenochtitlán. Situated at the empire's periphery and recently brought under Aztec control, the Totonacs were unwilling subjects of Montezuma. They were friendly to the Spanish strangers and impressed by their weapons and abilities. The Totonac chief took special interest in the Spanish show of power when Cortés seized and imprisoned Aztec tax collectors who had come to take Totonac prisoners for sacrifice. This daring act, which helped win the Totonacs as Spanish allies, also set the stage for later events Cortés would use as an excuse in taking Montezuma hostage.

Encouraged by Cortés's boldness against Montezuma's representatives, the Totonac chief told Cortés of the emperor's enemies.

Author Hugh Thomas recounts how the chief gave Cortés the idea that Montezuma could be defeated. After complaining of Aztec oppression,

> The chief also talked of the strength of Tenochtitlan and how, being built on the water, it was thought impregnable. But the people of Tlaxcala and Huexotzinco, as well as the Totonacs, hated the Mexica. [Prince] Ixtlilxochitl, the rival candidate for the throne of Texcoco, was also an enemy of Montezuma and, the chief thought, might help Cortés as well. The chief argued that if Cortés could make a league with these four peoples, Montezuma would be easily defeated.[15]

Thomas adds:

> The reason for the character of the welcome given by the chief was now obvious: he wanted a friend. The suggestion that the Castilians might ally themselves with the Totonacs and others against Montezuma gave Cortés for the first time an indication of how a serious onslaught against the Mexican empire might be made. For though he had aspired, for some time, to make a settlement on the coast, the idea of co-ordinating an alliance to fight Mexico itself seems not to have occurred to him before.[16]

With these interesting possibilities to consider, Cortés organized his men for the march to Montezuma's city. A number of Totonacs went with them as guides, and hundreds of porters were assigned to carry their equipment and provisions. It was mid-August 1519 when Cortés and his men set out for Tenochtitlán, which lay on the other side of high mountains that separated the coastal lowlands from the Valley of Mexico. About two-thirds of the way to the city, the Spanish would pass through the lands of the people that the Totonacs named as possible allies against Montezuma.

The Empire Contained Pockets of Resistance

A number of territories within the borders of the empire had refused to become tributary allies of the Aztecs, successfully defended themselves, and remained independent. The most important of these pockets of resistance was the land of Tlaxcala (also called Tlaxcallan), about sixty miles east of Tenochtitlán.

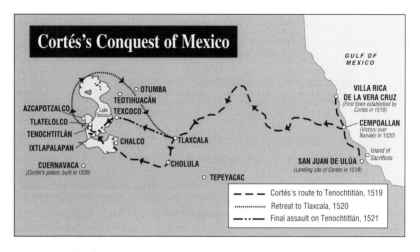

Ross Hassig explains the situation of the hostile Tlaxcalans (also called Tlaxcaltecs), longtime Aztec enemies, at the time the Spanish arrived: "The Tlaxcaltecs had been engaged in a series of wars with the Aztecs for decades, but now found themselves and their allies in a situation that continued to erode, completely encircled by Aztec tributaries and largely cut off from external trade. Without a profound alteration of the political situation, Tlaxcallan's defeat by the Aztecs was only a matter of time."[17]

Why the Aztecs had not yet subdued the Tlaxcalans when the Spanish arrived became a question in many minds. Montezuma told the conquistadors that he could have defeated the Tlaxcalans but purposely did not. Instead he claimed to be reserving this enemy as a target of ceremonial wars—or "flower" wars, as the Mexica called them—to take prisoners for sacrifice and to train warriors. Scholars suggest that this explanation was Montezuma's way of accounting for his inability to conquer these enemies or his unwillingness to pay the high price of casualties in the attempt. In any event, years of hostility fueled the hatred of these unconquered enemies, who would finally provide the Spanish with crucial support against Montezuma.

Cortés in Tlaxcala

The Tlaxcalans did not receive Cortés peacefully, however. Their animosity was at least partly because they believed the Spanish were friends of the Aztecs, since they were accompanied by Totonacs, who were known Aztec subjects. After days of bitter fighting in September,

Believing the Spanish to be allies of their longtime Aztec enemies, the Tlaxcalans met the Spanish soldiers with fierce resistance.

in which both the Tlaxcalans and the Spaniards suffered greatly, the Tlaxcalans made peace and offered to ally with the powerful strangers. In a report to the Spanish king, Cortés says, "I did not then leave the camp for six or seven days, for I dared not trust them, although they begged me to come to a great city of theirs where all the chiefs of the province are accustomed to live."[18]

During this week, Montezuma's emissaries who had accompanied the Spaniards tried to convince Cortés not to trust the Tlaxcalans, while the Tlaxcalans, in turn, warned him not to trust the Aztecs. Cortés revealed his understanding of the instability of the empire, writing, "When I saw the discord and animosity between these two peoples I was not a little pleased, for it seemed to further my purpose considerably; consequently, I might have the opportunity of subduing them more quickly, for, as the saying goes, 'divided they fall.'"[19] He went on to explain his strategy of setting the groups at odds, telling each one that he valued their friendship more than the other's.

Although not yet sure of the Tlaxcalans' trustworthiness, Cortés had made an ally of Montezuma's most committed enemies. And the Tlaxcalans, impressed with the military might of the Spaniards, had found a power that could aid their fight against the hated Aztecs. Sev-

eral thousand Tlaxcalans, in addition to the Totonacs, accompanied
Cortés and his men as they entered the core of Montezuma's empire.

Tenochtitlán: The Center of the Empire

The heart of the Aztec empire lay in the southern part of Lake Texcoco,
the biggest of the five shallow, connected lakes in the Valley of Mexico.
Here, on a small island, the Aztecs had founded their capital city, calling

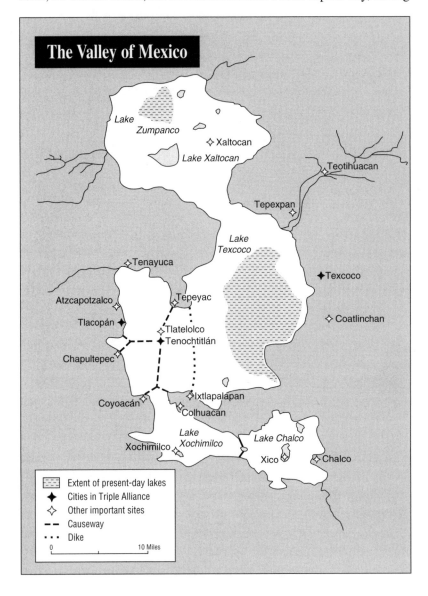

The Valley of Mexico

Lake Zumpanco
◇ Xaltocan
Lake Xaltocan
Teotihuacan
Tepexpan
Lake Texcoco
◇ Tenayuca
◆ Texcoco
Atzcapotzalco
Tepeyac
◇ Coatlinchan
Tlacopán ◆
◇ Tlatelolco
◆ Tenochtitlán
Chapultepec
◇ Ixtlapalápan
Coyoacán
Colhuacan
Lake Xochimilco
Lake Chalco
Xochimilco
Xico
◇ Chalco

Extent of present-day lakes
◆ Cities in Triple Alliance
◇ Other important sites
- - Causeway
• • • Dike
0   10 Miles

it Tenochtitlán. Over time the residents had enlarged the island, building up areas by bringing in earth, until they had built Tenochtitlán into a large and magnificent island city, crisscrossed by canals and connected to the mainland by three causeways.

Around the interconnected lakes were a number of cities and towns, constituting the powerful center of the Aztec empire. Some of these towns were older than Tenochtitlán, for the Aztecs were relative latecomers in the area, establishing their city less than two hundred years before the Spanish arrived. In 1519, Tenochtitlán headed the Triple Alliance, a coalition of cities comprising the older and important town of Texcoco on the east side of the lake and Tacuba (also called Tlacopán) on the western shore. After dominating Texcoco and Tacuba, the Aztecs had continued to extend their empire. Every year in the season of war, powerful armies left Tenochtitlán to conquer new areas or to subdue rebellious ones. And the mighty capital grew splendid with the riches that came to it from the tributary provinces. Large royal palaces, temple-topped pyramids, and busy markets made Tenochtitlán a lively center of imperial activity. The *pochteca*, the traveling merchants, brought back not only goods for the markets but also information for the emperor, for they served as Montezuma's eyes and ears on their travels.

Dissension at the Core of the Empire

Many people in the towns around the lakes were related by kinship and marriage ties. The Mexica, or Aztecs, are sometimes called the Culhua-Mexica, a name they adopted early in their history when they lived among members of the older town of Culhuacan on the western shore of the lake. As they established themselves in Tenochtitlán, they extended their kinship relationships to others in the area.

These towns around the lake, connected to the Aztecs by personal relationships, were the oldest parts of the empire. But even here, within the Triple Alliance itself, there were factions threatening to split alliances apart. Factions were often based on family disputes or loyalties. Daughters of one family were, for instance, often married to rulers of other families to create bonds between the groups. Since the people were polygynous, allowing some men to have more than one wife, competition for favor and power often developed among related groups and also could lead to disagreements and vio-

Large royal palaces and busy markets, accessible by canals, made Tenochtitlán a bustling center of imperial activity.

lence. The period following the death of a ruler was often a precarious time as well, because the throne did not automatically pass to a family member, such as the eldest surviving son; instead, the new emperor was selected from among several high-ranking candidates.

Tensions could also arise when an emperor interfered in local politics, hoping to build loyalty and cooperation by installing a ruler of his own choice. For example, after the death of the king of Texcoco, the second most powerful city in the Aztec empire, in 1515, Montezuma had installed his own nephew Cacama as the new king. But, in doing so, he had passed over several sons of the previous king, all legitimate heirs to Texcoco's throne. One of the rejected contenders was Ixtlilxochitl. This prince and his supporters had withdrawn from Texcoco, keeping a distant, but peaceful, relationship with Montezuma. The Totonac chief had suggested to Cortés that Ixtlilxochitl might help him in an alliance against the Aztecs. Ixtlilxochitl's help would not come until the final battle for Tenochtitlán, but this high-ranking noble's defection from the Triple Alliance reveals the lack of unity at the highest levels of Aztec leadership.

The Appearance of Weakness Invites Revolt

Factionalism, or divided loyalties, lay just under the surface in Montezuma's empire. In order to continue commanding the support of his subjects, the emperor had to appear strong. Any appearance of weakness encouraged rebellions or the shifting of allegiances as people supported political changes they thought would benefit them.

The process of selecting the Aztec emperor favored the strong. Each ruler had to be a warrior who had proven himself in battle. During the long coronation rites that confirmed the new emperor, he had to wage war and bring prisoners to sacrifice to the gods. A weak leader was not tolerated. At least once in Aztec history an emperor whose coronation war had not been successful was soon poisoned and replaced.

Within the requirements and expectations of his empire, Montezuma was a strong ruler. Richard F. Townsend, an expert on Aztec culture, states, "Motecuhzoma II was a notable warrior and his campaigns systematically enlarged the tribute domain and consolidated the network of conquests made by former rulers."[20] But when faced with the militarily powerful conquistadors, who provided a new focus for dissent, Montezuma and his empire began to falter. Unwilling subjects, unconquered enemies, and disaffected nobles all contributed to the instability of the empire Cortés would divide, weaken, and conquer.

Montezuma
Chapter 3   Does Not Resist

T HE SPANISH TROOPS ARRIVED at Tenochtitlán on November 8, 1519. Cortés and his men had been in Mexico for more than six months, and Montezuma had mounted no effective resistance against them. Scholars agree that the Aztecs, with their vastly superior numbers, could have succeeded in killing or driving off the small band of conquistadors. But Montezuma did not attack. Why the Aztec king did not use military force has puzzled historians, who suggest a variety of reasons to explain his behavior.

Montezuma Grants the Spaniards Diplomatic Status

Some believe that Montezuma remained peaceful toward the Spaniards because he accepted Cortés's claim to be an ambassador. According to scholar Anthony Pagden, "The attitude of the Mexica toward the Spaniards can best be explained by the traditional immunity from harm enjoyed by all ambassadors—and Cortés claimed to be an ambassador albeit without an embassy." [21]

Cortés's messages to Montezuma had stressed that he served a mighty king, Charles of Spain, who knew of Montezuma and had sent a delegation to see the Aztec ruler. The Aztecs were used to receiving diplomats and ambassadors. A visit from representatives of a foreign monarch would not have been out of the ordinary, even if the other king was unknown in Mexico.

Hugh Thomas writes that Montezuma's nephew Cacama, the new king of Texcoco, saw no harm in admitting the strangers. "'My advice,' he apparently said, 'is that, if you do not admit the embassy of a great lord such as the King of Spain appears to be, it is a low thing, since princes have the duty to hear the ambassadors of others.'"[22] Besides, he added shrewdly, there were warriors in the Aztec court to defend them if the ambassadors were false.

The Aztecs Were Unprepared for War

Another reason given for Montezuma's inaction is that the Aztec military was not ready for battle. Ross Hassig, an expert on Aztec warfare, points out that Montezuma may not have been convinced that he could mount a successful campaign against the powerful strangers at the time they arrived in Aztec territory. They had come in the month of June, two months after the Aztec army had disbanded for the agricultural season.

Also, says Hassig, Montezuma would not have been able to marshal a large army several months later when the Spanish had reached Tlaxcala and made allies of these enemies of the Aztecs. It was then harvest time, and it would be another two months before the Aztecs were free to mobilize for the traditional war season.

Meanwhile, the conquistadors had demonstrated astounding military strength in their battles with the Tlaxcalans, before the two groups became allies. Without his fully mobilized army, the Aztec emperor had only a small military force. According to Hassig, "Moteuczoma did have a corps of elite soldiers—perhaps a few thousand—but these were too few for an assault against the Spaniards and their allies in distant Tlaxcallan."[23]

Montezuma Was Frightened by Ill Omens

Some reports suggest yet another reason for Montezuma's inaction: The emperor's reluctance to face Cortés grew out of fears based on ill omens. Scholar David Carrasco writes, "The indigenous accounts of the conquest tell that omens of great portent appeared in the Valley of Mexico a full decade before Cortés arrived."[24]

Omens were important to the Aztecs, and when such signs appeared, the emperor's priests, advisers, and magicians were responsible for interpreting them. For some of the omens, it was impossible to find a favorable interpretation. For example, a temple of Huitzilopochtli, main god of the Aztecs and a symbol of the emperor's authority, was destroyed in a fire said to have been started by a bolt of lightning from a clear blue sky.

Montezuma

Montezuma became the emperor of the Aztecs in 1502. He was an accomplished warrior who led many campaigns to expand the territory of Aztec control. But he had also failed to subdue the Tlaxcalans in several

The soft-spoken Montezuma believed in using fear to rule his empire.

wars and, likewise, had not won the war he initiated with the Tarascans north of the Valley of Mexico. After one disastrous battle with the Tlaxcalans, he had punished his unsuccessful warriors by not allowing them to wear the dress customary for their rank for a year.

Early in his reign he moved to consolidate his support among the nobles. He introduced social changes that made it more difficult for commoners to achieve status. He refused to have commoners as servants, reserving these positions of honor for nobles, including the young princes of tributary towns who lived in the capital for education and training. Many of the exaggerated signs of respect toward the emperor that the Spaniards saw, such as not looking at Montezuma's face, were practices he himself had started.

Before he was the emperor, Montezuma had been a high priest and was thoroughly familiar with the methods of divination that the Aztecs used to help them in making difficult decisions. He tried—without success—to rely on these methods for interpretations of celestial omens and advice about how to deal with the Spaniards. It is said that diviners and magicians whose answers did not please him were put to death.

When Cortés arrived, Montezuma was about fifty years old and had ruled for seventeen years. He was said to be courteous in manner, soft-spoken, and eloquent in speech. He also had a reputation for being rigid. According to one conquistador, he told Cortés that the way to rule was through fear.

According to the native sources, the negative portents troubled Montezuma greatly. When Grijalva's expedition appeared in 1518, the emperor had feared that these strangers were, or might be, the threat of which the omens warned. When Cortés and his men arrived the following year, Montezuma's fears apparently intensified until he was incapable of choosing a course of action.

Montezuma Might Have Thought the Spaniards Were Gods

The earliest and most popular reason given for Montezuma's nonresistance, however, is that he believed Cortés was the god Quetzalcoatl returning to reclaim the Aztec lands. This idea began to circulate within a decade after the conquest.

Quetzalcoatl was a legendary god-king of the Toltecs, a powerful earlier people whose ruined capital of Tula (Tollan) was located north of Tenochtitlán. This god-king was forced to leave his city during a dispute with other gods and was said to have departed on a raft toward the Yucatán in the east. In the version of the legend told after

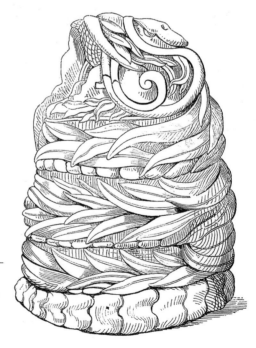

Quetzalcoatl is depicted here as a feathered serpent. This ancient god-king's name is one of the titles of Aztec rulers.

the conquest, Quetzalcoatl promised to return. Since the Aztecs saw themselves as the heirs to Toltec civilization, their lands would be the ones reclaimed by the returning god.

This version of the Quetzalcoatl legend is similar to another story reported by Cortés in an account to the Spanish king. The second tale features not the god but a lord, or culture-hero, who supposedly led the Mexica to Tenochtitlán and taught them the arts of civilization. This lord left his followers on the island, and when he returned for them, they had settled down and no longer wanted to follow him. He left again but promised that some day his descendants would return to claim their land. Cortés wrote to Charles of Spain that Montezuma said he believed the Spanish were those lost lords the Aztecs had always known would return.

These two stories—the legend of the god-king who disappeared into the east and the tale of returning lords—apparently merged very early into the one legend of the returning Quetzalcoatl. Soon after the conquest, Montezuma's supposed belief that Cortés was the reincarnation of Quetzalcoatl began to be accepted as the reason why the king did not resist the Spanish.

New Interpretations

More recently, however, scholars have questioned whether the legend of the returning Quetzalcoatl even existed before the conquest. Historian Nigel Davies, an expert in Aztec culture and beliefs, finds no evidence that such a prophecy existed in any native sources before the Spaniards arrived. For this reason, he believes that, after the conquest, the original legend about the god was changed to include the prediction that the god would return.

Anthropologist/archaeologist Susan Gillespie explains why the Aztecs might change the legend in this way. Pointing out that the Aztecs looked to the past to explain events of the present, she says the story of the returning Quetzalcoatl was created by Aztec elders in an attempt to understand the conquest. As they tried to make events fit a pattern of happenings or expectations from their own culture, they looked among their gods and heroes to find one whose actions were similar to those of Cortés. Since Quetzalcoatl was said to have gone off into the east, the direction from which Cortés came, the Spanish captain general became associated with Quetzalcoatl.

An Aztec Idea of Gods

The conquistador Bernal Díaz, among others, stated that the natives called them *teules,* his Spanish rendition of the Nahuatl term *teotl.* He says it was their word for god or demon. The following explanation by Richard F. Townsend, in his book *The Aztecs,* is helpful in understanding how the Aztecs themselves understood the term.

> A basic concept of Aztec religious thought was expressed by the word-root *teo,* often written with the *tl* suffix as *teotl.* Difficult to translate, the word was recorded by the Spanish as "god," "saint," or sometimes "demon." Studies of the word *teo* show that it appears in Nahuatl texts in a variety of contexts. Sometimes it accompanies the names of nature-deities, but it was also used in connection with human impersonators of those divinities, as well as in association with their sacred masks and related ceremonial objects, including sculptured effigies of wood, stone, or dough. Such words as "mana," "numinous" or "sacred" have been used to suggest its significance.

> Townsend goes on to say that the Aztecs might also use this word to describe almost anything outside their ordinary experience, whether good or evil. The word could be connected, for example, with fearsome animals, life-sustaining or -threatening forces of nature, or even great leaders.

> The many different ways in which the Aztecs used this word reflect their belief that extraordinary power might appear anywhere. Thus, in the Aztec worldview, inanimate objects might have a life force, human beings could manifest godlike characteristics, and gods might intervene in human affairs.

Richard F. Townsend supports these recent interpretations: "Given that the Aztecs viewed history as a cycle of repeated events, it is highly plausible that their historians should have sought to rewrite the past in this way."[25] He concludes that it is doubtful that Montezuma truly believed Cortés was the returning god, although he may have considered this possibility, among others.

Ross Hassig points out that, since the Aztecs believed that gods interacted with humans, it would have been compatible with Aztec beliefs for Montezuma to entertain the possibility that the conquistadors were gods. As he says,

> The Spaniards were unlike any people seen before and they had technological capabilities that seemed godlike, so a supernatural origin had to be considered, especially in the

Aztec worldview where gods could play direct roles in human affairs. After considerable thought and discussion, the notion that the strangers might be gods was accepted—not, apparently, as a fact, but as a disturbing possibility.[26]

The Aztecs Develop a Strategy

What Montezuma actually thought cannot be known with certainty. To help him decide how to respond to the arrival of the mysterious strangers, Montezuma consulted with his council of leaders.

Some did not share the emperor's uncertainty. Montezuma's brother Cuitláhuac and his cousin Cuauhtémoc, each of whom would later become emperor, took a different view. From the beginning, they thought the Spanish were simply powerful invaders who should be resisted. Others supported the emperor in his reluctance to take military action, and apparently Montezuma's doubts swayed the decision. The course of action, however, was not one dictated by the emperor alone, for despite the Aztec ruler's near-dictatorial powers, he needed the support of other Aztec leaders to maintain his political position. As Ross Hassig writes,

> Between the landings of Grijalva and Cortés, Moteuczoma had consulted with his priests and advisers: how the Spaniards should be treated was not his decision alone, but was also the considered opinion of his counsellors. Moteuczoma probably played a major, if not pivotal, role in deciding to take no action, but this decision was one in which all the advisers had a stake, and not even the king could disregard or change it without risking his political support.[27]

Montezuma and his counselors agreed that the strangers should be given whatever they wanted, but they should not be permitted to come to Tenochtitlán. This was a strategy more easily devised than accomplished. The magicians' spells sent to the coast did not succeed in chasing off the strangers. And the emperor's best gifts did not satisfy the Spanish desire for gold. Despite Montezuma's numerous orders that the Spanish not come to Tenochtitlán, Cortés continued to march inland.

Did the Aztecs Attempt to Stop Cortés?

Once the conquistadors were within about three days' march of the capital, according to Cortés, Montezuma made two attempts to stop them. Modern historians are not certain what happened. Perhaps the Aztec emperor had made an exception to his strategy of nonresistance as the Spaniards drew near. Or possibly the events did not happen as Cortés described them.

The first attempt, Cortés says, was an ambush planned to take place outside the city of Cholula, an Aztec ally, where warriors were said to be waiting to intercept the Spanish as they departed the town. When the plot was reported to Cortés, he and his own men struck first, trapping and killing thousands of unarmed Cholulans in the courtyard of the city's temple to Quetzalcoatl.

Whether the threat of Aztec ambush was real or fabricated, Cortés had good strategic reasons to attack Cholula, which lay on the Spaniards' route back to the coast. Since the massacre killed thousands of men, the city's ability to fight was weakened, and the Spanish victory allowed Cortés to influence the choice of Cholula's new ruler and install a leader friendly to himself. The brutal and unexpected attack also served to terrorize the Aztecs.

The second attempt to stop the Spanish, according to Cortés, was a trick to lure them onto a certain mountain road where warriors were waiting to attack. This plot was foiled, he said, when local townspeople betrayed the trap and the Spaniards took another route.

Montezuma Permits Cortés to Enter Tenochtitlán

Cortés sent harsh messages to Montezuma, complaining of the alleged ambushes and restating his intention to come to Tenochtitlán. According to native sources, Montezuma was increasingly agitated as the Spanish approached and fearful when he heard that Cortés believed he had been treacherous. Yet, along with reprimands, Cortés continued to assure Montezuma that he was coming as a friend.

Conquistador Bernal Díaz says, "We heard that when Montezuma learned that we did not lay all the blame on him, he fasted and sacrificed to his idols in an effort to learn whether he should permit us to enter his city. The answer was that he should allow us to enter, since once we were inside, he could kill us whenever he wished."[28]

At last, the Aztec emperor invited Cortés to enter the capital. While Montezuma may have had several reasons for allowing Cortés into his city, one of the main ones was political. By befriending Cortés himself, the Aztec king would keep any other contenders for power from joining forces with the Spanish against him. As Ross Hassig observes, "He knew about the massacre at Cholollan [Cholula] and that the new king had assumed power with Spanish help and that his own politically divided city and region also harbored dissident factions. Any opposition to Cortés could embolden these groups and threaten his position, so Moteuczoma was conciliatory."[29]

Unarmed Cholulans run in terror as Cortés's soldiers launch a brutal attack.

Hassig continues,

Perhaps Moteuczoma did want Cortés inside Tenochtitlán where he could be seized and killed, or perhaps he was biding his time until the war season, when he could again raise a large army and deal with the Spaniards as well as the Tlaxcaltecs and all the rebellious provinces to the east. But whatever the king's motivations, Cortés did enter Tenochtitlán where Moteuczoma embraced him, which would have stilled any public rifts among the Aztec rulers and nobles.[30]

Cortés Takes Montezuma Hostage

Montezuma treated the Spanish as guests, giving them quarters in the large palace of an earlier king located near his own residence in the main public area of the city. The conquistadors quickly realized the danger they

Montezuma welcomes Cortés and his entourage, unaware that the course of Aztec history would soon change forever.

When Montezuma and Cortés First Met

Conquistador Bernal Díaz described the first meeting of Cortés and Montezuma. The leaders met in a formal ceremony on the main causeway into Tenochtitlán, with Montezuma approaching the Spaniards in a litter.

When we came close to Mexico, at a place where there were other, smaller towers, Montezuma descended from his litter while these great chiefs supported him with their arms beneath a marvelously rich canopy of green feathers, worked with gold and silver, pearl and *chalchiuis*, which hung from a kind of border that was wonderful to see. He was richly dressed and wore shoes like sandals, with soles of gold covered with precious stones. The four chiefs who supported him were also richly dressed, in clothes that had apparently been held ready for them on the road, for they had not worn them when they received us. There were four other chiefs who carried the canopy and many other lords who walked before the great Montezuma, sweeping the ground where he would pass, and putting down mats so that he would not have to walk on the ground. None of these lords thought of looking in his face; all of them kept their eyes down, with great reverence.

When Cortés saw the great Montezuma approaching, he jumped from his horse and they showed great respect toward each other. Montezuma welcomed him, and through Doña Marina, Cortés replied that he hoped that Montezuma was in good health. It seems to me that Cortés offered his right hand, and that Montezuma did not take it, but he did give his hand to Cortés.

Then Cortés gave him a necklace he had ready at hand, made of the glass stones that I have already called margaritas, which have in them many designs and a variety of colors. They were strung on a golden cord and sweetly scented with musk. He placed it around Montezuma's neck and was going to embrace him when the princes accompanying him caught Cortés by the arm so that he could not do so, for they thought it an indignity.

Through Doña Marina, Cortés said he rejoiced at meeting so great a prince, and Montezuma answered politely and commanded his nephews to show us to our quarters.

were in. The island city was connected to the mainland by three long causeways built of earth and stone. These narrow strips of land were cut through in places by channels, crossed by wooden bridges. If the bridges were lifted to close off the causeways, the Spanish, having no boats or canoes, would be stranded in the city.

To forestall being trapped and to acquire leverage over the Aztecs by demonstrating control of their ruler, Cortés devised a plan to take Montezuma hostage. He and his men would pretend to pay a social call. Because Montezuma had permitted Cortés and his captains, fully armed, to come and go freely from his presence, their visit to capture him, hardly a week after their arrival, would not arouse suspicion.

Cortés had found a reason to give the emperor as to why he must become a prisoner. It involved the Totonacs, the coastal people Cortés had freed from paying tribute to the Aztecs when he had seized Montezuma's tax collectors. Now, five months later, Aztec representatives were again trying to collect tribute from the Totonacs, and fighting erupted when Spaniards from the garrison at Villa Rica went to aid their allies. Cortés had just received word that several Spaniards had been killed; he used this news to accuse Montezuma of treachery. Although the emperor denied ordering the actions and promised to punish the Aztec officials involved, Cortés insisted that Montezuma must come and stay with the Spaniards in their quarters until the situation could be resolved. Montezuma protested the indignity but at last was convinced that he must accompany the conquistadors or be killed.

This daring act of capture succeeded—at least partly—because the Aztecs had been completely unprepared for it; not even the most wary adviser had foreseen that such an affront would be offered to the revered person of the emperor. Native sources later recalled that this astounding action by Cortés terrified the people of Tenochtitlán.

To save face and keep his servants and officials from resisting on his behalf, the emperor pretended that he was going of his own free will to spend some time with the Spanish in their quarters. Montezuma's cooperation with the Spanish at this point is another mystery historians have attempted to explain. Hassig observes, "Why Moteuczoma would cooperate is puzzling, but he did; fear for his own personal safety is a less likely explanation than fear for his political future."[31] If he were seen as weak, or if people realized that he was being held against his will, others would try to replace him on the throne.

Montezuma Is Imprisoned

Montezuma's imprisonment was a great crisis for Tenochtitlán. But for a while, at least on the surface, all went on as usual. Though confined to the Spanish quarters, the emperor continued to receive his officials and give orders for the government of the city. And he continued to make sacrifices and consult his gods for guidance.

However, he was always attended by armed Spanish guards so that his position as a hostage was clear. Hugh Thomas remarks, "Most noblemen of Mexico were neither deceived nor amused. Many refused to go and see Montezuma in his 'prison.'"[32] The native sources say that the people no longer listened to him and that the city was afraid.

As months passed, Montezuma's power waned. Even the semi-sacred authority of the emperor's office could not keep the nobles loyal when the Spaniards moved against Aztec religion, tearing

A soldier shackles Montezuma to prevent him from escaping as the Aztec leader is taken hostage by the Spanish.

down the statues of Aztec gods in the main temples and replacing
them with likenesses of the Virgin Mary and Christian saints. As Hassig notes, "Cortés controlled Moteuczoma but he lacked a full understanding of the nature and limits of the king's power. Moteuczoma's tenure in office depended on proper actions, yet most of what
he ordered at Cortés's insistence was contrary to Aztec interests and
his support among both the people and the nobility eroded."[33]

Cortés Faces Problems on Multiple Fronts

Sometime in March, Cortés was warned by Montezuma that he and
his men should leave before they were attacked. According to Hugh
Thomas, the Mexica, led by members of Tenochtitlán's council, had
been making efforts to get military help from their allies. "A serious
effort was thus under way to assemble a new Mexican army, even
though the season for war, as laid down in the calendars, had passed,
and though the whole chain of command had been interrupted by the
Castilians' imprisonment of the Emperor."[34] In response to Montezuma's warning, Cortés told the emperor that the Spaniards would
leave as soon as their men on the coast had built ships, since the vessels they came in had been grounded when they arrived.

Soon, however, circumstances changed, both in Tenochtitlán and
at Villa Rica, on the coast. In early May, Cortés received word that
an expedition of Spaniards had arrived with orders from Governor
Velázquez to arrest him and return him to Cuba. Disturbed by reports
that Cortés had founded Villa Rica and was attempting to conquer
and settle lands that the governor himself wanted to colonize,
Velázquez had sent troops to stop the captain general, charging him
with the crime of insubordination for overstepping the mission the
governor had granted him. The new expedition, led by Pánfilo de
Narváez, included hundreds of men. Leaving about a hundred men
under the command of Pedro de Alvarado at Tenochtitlán, Cortés,
with a group of 350 soldiers, left to confront Narváez. In the ensuing
military encounter, Narváez was defeated, and with bribes and
promises of gold, Cortés recruited several hundred of Narváez's men
to his command.

Meanwhile, the Spanish troops left at the capital had come under
siege. While Cortés was away, Alvarado had ordered the massacre of
thousands of unarmed Mexican nobles assembled to celebrate the

festival of Toxcatl, one of the year's most important religious events. At last the people of the city rose up against the Spaniards, who took refuge in their fortified quarters. Only the use of cannons and guns held off the Aztecs.

From the palace roof, Montezuma asked his people to stop the attack. He still had enough influence to halt the worst of the fighting, but, reportedly, he said, "Alvarado, if you had not begun it, my men would not have done this. You have ruined yourselves and me also."[35] Killing thousands of Tenochtitlán's best warriors was a military victory for the Spanish and may have helped them survive in the later flight from the city, but the act raised the ire of the Aztecs against both the Spanish and their imprisoned leader.

Cortés and his soldiers leave Tenochtitlán to confront Narváez, who was sent by Governor Velázquez to arrest Cortés and return him to Cuba.

The Aztecs Fight Back

Trapped in the palace with little food and water, the conquistadors continued to hold out until Cortés returned on June 24. Reinforced with the soldiers from Narváez's expedition, Cortés's troops entered Tenochtitlán unopposed. They found the city in mourning and the markets closed. When asked to have the markets reopened, Montezuma said he no longer had influence over the people. But he suggested that Cortés release his brother Cuitláhuac with instructions to open the markets so that the Spanish could get provisions.

"As soon as this prince was free," writes Hugh Thomas, "he began urgently to organise the Mexican resistance. Whether he was formally elected emperor of the Mexicans at this time is obscure. It is also unclear whether Montezuma realised the implications of what he was doing. But thenceforward the Mexica possessed a warlord."[36] Cuitláhuac had been opposed to the Spanish from the beginning. Now, under his leadership, the Mexica announced their intention to fight to the death.

Within a week, the Spanish were losing so badly that they again sought Montezuma's help in controlling the Aztecs. But this time, as soon as the emperor appeared on the rooftop, he was struck by stones thrown from the crowd. By the next day, he was dead; whether he died from the wound or was killed by the Spanish as they prepared to flee the city is unknown.

The Spanish Flight

The Spanish planned a retreat by night, leaving Tenochtitlán by the shortest causeway, which led west to Tacuba. Many soldiers carried gold bars, formed from melted-down Aztec treasures, because there was too much gold to be carried by the horses alone. When the retreating Spaniards were discovered, the Aztecs attacked fiercely by land and from canoes. In this "Noche Triste," or "Sad Night," as the Spanish called June 30, 1520, two-thirds of the conquistadors died. Most of the horses died as well, and much of the gold, including the "royal fifth," the Spanish king's allotment, was lost. Many Spaniards were killed by Aztec warriors, but many also drowned in channels where bridges had been taken up. Some, especially if they were not weighted down by gold, saved themselves by swimming. Those Spaniards who reached the mainland fought their way toward the north.

The Aztecs soon gave up serious attempts to pursue the enemy and returned to Tenochtitlán to celebrate their victory and deal with their losses. Although with Montezuma dead there was no authoritative

Montezuma is struck by arrows and stones delivered by his own people, angry with him for surrendering to the Spanish.

The battle called the "Sad Night" by Spaniards claimed the lives of two-thirds of the conquistadors.

voice urging Aztec restraint, the Aztec leaders did not press their advantage over the small band of exhausted and wounded conquistadors. Had they persisted in the attack, they might well have destroyed the Spaniards. Such failure to persevere in battle was a mistake the Aztecs would repeat, to their misfortune, in other encounters with the Spanish.

Weapons, Warfare, and Leadership

WITH MONTEZUMA DEAD AND the Aztecs vowing to resist the Spaniards, the struggle for control of the empire depended entirely on military success. When they met on the battlefield, the two sides used different weapons and employed different approaches to fighting. Superior weapons and more advanced techniques of warfare, coupled with Cortés's brilliant leadership, gave the Spaniards an edge the Aztecs were never able to overcome.

The Advantage of Spanish Weapons

Spanish weapons were technologically more advanced than those of the Aztecs. Spanish steel swords did not shatter as native stone swords might, and their edges remained sharp longer. Importantly, they could wound by a forward thrust as well as by side-to-side slashing. According to Bernal Díaz, most of the natives killed in battle died from puncture wounds caused by sword thrusts.

Spanish crossbows shot farther and more forcefully than the simple bows used by the natives. In addition, the Spaniards had hand-held firearms called harquebuses. Since crossbows and harquebuses had greater ranges than the native slings and bows did, the Spaniards could fire into the advancing Aztecs and disrupt their formations while remaining out of range of the natives' simpler projectile weapons.

Besides harquebuses, the Spanish had several small cannon. Firearms, like horses and war dogs, were new to the Aztecs. The terror these weapons inspired gave the Spanish an added advantage, for native troops sometimes fled at the sight of the horsemen or the firing cannon. It took time for the Aztecs to learn how to react to these unfamiliar

weapons. Meanwhile, the Spanish won battles and built a reputation as
strong warriors. Even though the Spaniards also had to accustom themselves to unfamiliar warfare, including the loud and frightening native
war calls, most conquistadors had already experienced Indian warfare

*The Spaniard's superior weapons, such as the steel sword, gave them an
edge over their Aztec opponents.*

by the time they encountered the Aztecs, whereas groups of Aztecs were often fighting Spaniards for the first time.

The Advantage of Horses

The Spanish horses gave the conquistadors one of their greatest fighting advantages. A horseman, armed with a long lance and charging into the ranks of the opposing army, could strike many enemies, often without being struck in return. The horses, like the conquistadors themselves, were protected by metal armor. With speed and force, even a small cavalry unit of only five or six horses could break open the orderly lines of the Aztecs, allowing Spanish swordsmen to move in swiftly and engage the enemy troops while they were in disarray.

The Spanish were quick to exploit the natives' fear of horses. For example, Cortés often made a show of the animals, demonstrating

 The Importance of the Spanish Sword

Although the Spaniards had some crossbows and firearms, most of their soldiers fought with steel swords. At times, especially in their most desperate circumstances, the Spanish had exhausted their arrows and gunpowder and the fighting relied on swords alone. In his book *The Aztec Empire*, Nigel Davies, historian of Aztec history and culture, gives much credit for the conquest to the superiority of this conventional weapon.

> The Spanish ability to defeat any number of Indians in the open field probably owed more to the superior quality of their more conventional weapons: the bow and in particular the sword, the equivalent in hand-to-hand fighting of the native club. The crossbow completely outmatched the Aztec bow, though it was a rather cumbersome weapon, slow to load and less effective in wet weather; it had proved inferior to the English longbow at the battle of Crecy, 173 years before the Conquest! Of greater significance was the Spanish sword, with which most of the Spanish force was armed; it was wholly superior to the native club, which had to be lifted head-high to inflict a blow, whereas the conquerors could dispatch Aztec after Aztec with lightning sword thrusts before they could strike back with their more unwieldy arm. The sword was the decisive weapon in the fatal battle of Otumba.

Although at Otumba the Spaniards had only their swords and a few horses, the foot soldiers had managed to defend themselves until Cortés's daring charge into the midst of the Aztec army killed the native leader and caused the Aztec troops to disperse.

their power and speed whenever the Spaniards encountered new groups of natives. Once he used them when he saw the enemy moving into position for a night attack, which he feared would put his men at a disadvantage. Cortés reports, "I therefore determined to ride

A Spanish horseman slays Aztec warriors during the Battle of Otumba, where the use of horses was instrumental to the Spaniards' victory.

out to meet them with all the horsemen to frighten and scatter them so they would be unable to reach the camp."[37] This maneuver succeeded in driving the natives away.

Horses were used to their best advantage in open spaces where they could move freely, turn, and charge again. When battles were fought in unconfined areas, the horses were often instrumental in winning. Nowhere was this better demonstrated than at the desperate battle of Otumba, fought several days after the Spanish fled Tenochtitlán on the Noche Triste.

Horses at the Battle of Otumba

The Spanish forces that survived the Noche Triste numbered fewer than four hundred soldiers and thirty horses. Most of the men and animals were wounded. As the conquistadors made their way north around the lake, headed toward Tlaxcala, they fought off Aztec attackers daily. But the Aztecs failed to mount a sustained assault until the retreating Spaniards reached the town of Otumba several days later, around July 6.

The large Aztec army gathered at Otumba engaged the Spaniards in fierce fighting for hours, until the conquistadors, already wounded and tired, were failing from fatigue. With such small numbers, the Spaniards could not allow any men to rest, whereas the numerous Aztecs could replace warriors with fresh troops. Realizing that he was losing the battle, Cortés responded with a daring move that could be carried out only on horseback. He and several other horsemen, armed with lances, rode through the surprised Mexica to attack and kill their leader, who was easily identified by the large, colorful standard he wore. Once the leader fell and the standard could not be seen, the Aztecs lost direction and scattered.

The battle at Otumba is considered one of the turning points in the conquest of Mexico, giving the conquistadors a victory at a time when the Aztecs could have destroyed them. A statue of Cortés, with the name of Otumba on it, stands in the conquistador's home province of Medellín, Spain, to recall the event. Writer Hugh Thomas points out that "There should also be a statue there to the horse of Castile. For if ever that animal turned the day in a battle, it was on this occasion."[38]

Cortés himself underlined the importance of horses and the more advanced Spanish weapons to his cause. He told the king of Spain that horses, arms, crossbows, and gunpowder are what he most needed in fighting the Aztecs, observing that the foot soldiers alone could not win battles because they were outnumbered.

The Aztecs' Superior Numbers Are Not Enough

The Aztecs indeed had vastly superior numbers. Spanish estimates of the number of opponents they faced in battle range from thousands to tens of thousands, but there are no ways to verify these numbers. It is known, however, that the Aztec army was organized in units of one hundred to four hundred men drawn from local towns. These units were combined into larger fighting forces of eight thousand men. Twenty-five such units, totaling two hundred thousand men drawn

 ## Aztecs Rely on Numbers for Superiority

When the Aztecs fought with other Indians, both sides used the same kinds of weapons and tactics. Aztec victories, on which they had built their empire, depended mostly on mounting a larger force than their enemies'. The Aztecs themselves relied on this, telling the Spaniards that eventually they would win because there were so many of them. Other natives also warned Cortés that he could not stand up to the greatly superior Aztec numbers. One of them was a Totonac chief who had accompanied the Spanish on their march inland. His warning came as Cortés prepared to leave Tlaxcala for Tenochtitlán. The chief's words were recorded by one of Cortés's captains, conquistador Andrés de Tapia, and appear in *The Conquistadors*, edited by Patricia de Fuentes.

> He said to the marques: "Sire, do not trouble yourself going on from here. As a youth I went to Mexico, and am experienced in the wars. I know that you and your companions are men and not gods; that you hunger and thirst and weary as men do. Let it be known to you that beyond this province lie so many people, that one hundred thousand men will fight you now, and when these are dead or vanquished, that many again will come forward, and again and again by the hundred thousand, and you and yours, though you be invincible, will die wearied of fighting. For as I have told you, I know you are men, and all I can say is that you should think carefully about what I have said. But if you determine to die, then I shall go with you."

With characteristic boldness and determination, Cortés answered that he would continue on, knowing that God would help them, and he urged the chief to believe the same. Both Totonacs and Tlaxcalans accompanied Cortés as he went on to meet Montezuma in the Aztec capital.

from throughout the empire, were said to have been used on Aztec long-distance expeditions. Given units of these sizes, it is reasonable to assume that the small band of fewer than five hundred Spaniards routinely faced thousands of warriors in a single encounter.

The Aztecs' superior numbers put the Spanish in most danger when they were trapped in Tenochtitlán, for the city was estimated to have perhaps forty-five thousand men of military service age. When Cortés reported that the Aztec leaders had vowed to fight to the death, he added, "Furthermore they had calculated that if 25,000 of them died for every one of us, they would finish with us first, for they were many and we were but few."[39] Once he had escaped the city, Cortés immediately sought to undercut the Aztecs' advantage by choosing a route to the north through poorly populated areas, where any armies drawn from local towns would not be large. This strategy worked for several days, until the conquistadors had to face the large body of Aztecs at Otumba. Had the Aztecs not fled the field after their leader fell but instead continued to send fresh warriors against the Spaniards until the conquistadors were too exhausted to resist, there is little doubt that their superior numbers would have destroyed the enemy, even in the face of superior arms and Spanish horses. But the Aztecs did not sustain their attacks until the Spanish were incapable of fighting back, either at Otumba or in any other encounter. Time after time, they outnumbered the Spaniards, yet their superior numbers did not bring them victory in battle.

The Spanish Have Superior Discipline and Organization

Besides their advanced weapons, the Spanish had the advantage of more disciplined methods of fighting. The natives, for example, tended to stop fighting when their leader was killed or captured. Even when this occurred early in a battle, or when the Aztecs were close to defeating the Spaniards, as they were at Otumba, native troops habitually dispersed after their leader was killed.

The Aztecs were also handicapped in battle with the Spanish because of their custom of taking live captives for sacrifice. Since capturing enemy warriors to serve as human sacrifices was a primary goal of native warfare, Aztec warriors were often more concerned with taking captives than with killing an enemy outright. In addition, since the advancement of warriors, both in military and social status, depended on the numbers

Aztec Warriors and Warfare

Since their empire was dependent on warfare, the Aztecs had a strong tradition of military training. Boys received basic training in warfare, whether they attended *telpochcalli* schools, directed by leaders of the neighborhoods in which they lived, or *calmecac* schools, which were temple schools run by priests. Military instruction began at about the age of fifteen and appears to have been more rigorous in the temple schools, attended primarily by nobles but also by commoners who aspired to a military career.

Further training was carried out under the direction of veteran warriors, such as the eagle and jaguar knights, who were quartered in the king's palace and provided troops ready for action. These accomplished warriors, who had taken many captives, wore special insignia and particular kinds of dress according to their rank and status. They fought with finely crafted obsidian or flint-edged swords, spears, and clubs that crushed, cut, and slashed opponents in hand-to-hand combat.

Most soldiers in the Aztec armies, however, were farmers or artisans who served as auxiliary troops during the war season. They had to be mobilized for war, provided with weapons (primarily slings and bows and arrows), and sometimes given refresher training sessions. An Aztec attack typically began with a hail of stones or arrows slung or shot from a distance into the advancing enemy army. As the opposing forces drew nearer, more specialized fighters might use the *atlatl*, a throwing stick that imparted speed and force to the darts it threw. These various projectile weapons helped to break up the orderly formation of the enemy troops.

As opposing armies met, the elite warriors, sometimes protected with thick, quilted cotton armor, moved forward to engage the enemy in hand-to-hand combat. Apparently, it was the encounters of these elite soldiers, fighting at the front lines, that determined the outcome of battles, for if they began to lose, or if a leader was killed or captured, the rest of the army often dispersed, considering the battle lost.

and ranks of the captives they took, Aztec men often tended to fight as individuals pursuing personal goals.

In contrast, the conquistadors fought in tightly organized formations, protecting fellow soldiers. Their discipline and organization were based on the most advanced European military methods. Nigel Davies notes,

> The Spaniards were the greatest soldiers of the age, and for a century and a half no Spanish army was ever defeated in a pitched battle. Under such circumstances numbers hardly counted. In the open field a handful of Spaniards could make

mincemeat of a horde of Indians who were trying to fight such a formidable adversary by engaging in a conflict that was indeed war, but of a kind never wholly free of an element of ritual or magic; the Indians simply did not understand the meaning of total war as it was conducted in sixteenth-century Europe. They were always inhibited by their urge to capture rather than to kill.[40]

Cortés, a Skillful Leader

Along with advanced weapons and superior battle discipline, the Spanish had a brilliant, daring, and determined leader in Cortés. He was able to understand the situations in which the Spanish found themselves and improvise ways to exploit those situations to their

Veteran Aztec warriors wore special attire according to their rank and status. This jaguar knight wears a helmet in the likeness of a jaguar's head and carries a wooden sword edged with sharp stone.

advantage. He had not only military skills but also political and diplomatic skills, helping him to find and keep allies among the natives. To convince people to join his cause, he used shows of power, promising aid if they joined with him and threatening reprisal and punishment if they did not.

Cortés aggressively worked to create an image of strength. For example, when he seized Montezuma's tax collectors, he presented himself as being powerful enough to challenge the emperor's authority. At every opportunity, he encouraged the natives to believe that the Spaniards were superior, both on the battlefield and in personal characteristics. On one occasion, when Montezuma remarked that the Spaniards must be tired after accompanying him on the long climb to the top of a temple pyramid, Cortés responded that he and his men were never tired.

Even when it was a hardship to spare men and horses, Cortés kept up his show of strength by supporting allies who requested help. This support was crucial, for once a native group had allied with the Spaniards, it was vulnerable to Aztec retaliation. Cortés took care to maintain his coalition by making it worthwhile for his allies to remain loyal.

Distrust of the Aztecs Helps the Spanish

While Cortés had worked to impress his new allies with his strength and reliability, the Aztecs had developed a reputation for lies and treachery. Many natives, both subjects and enemies of the Aztecs, did not trust them. This suspicion helped the Spanish cause because it kept the natives from joining in a united front against them. Had they been able to overcome their suspicion of the Aztecs, the other natives of Mexico might have recognized that the Spanish were a threat to them all.

It was partly fear of Aztec treachery that kept the Tlaxcalans from deserting their alliance with Cortés after the Noche Triste. At that time, the Aztecs offered a truce, seeking to reconcile with their old enemies and unite against the Spaniards, whom they now saw as the enemy of all natives. While some Tlaxcalan leaders also saw the Spanish threat, others were afraid to trust Aztec intentions and promises, and their final decision was to stick with their alliance with Cortés.

The Aztecs' past behavior also kept them from getting aid from the Tarascans (Purépecha) of adjoining Michoacán. The Aztecs had tried, unsuccessfully, to defeat these neighbors to the north, who remained independent. Later, when Cuauhtémoc, the last Aztec emperor, asked the Tarascans for help, their leader, too, feared a trick and refused to join in a coalition against the Spanish. "With that decision," observes Hugh Thomas, "he probably sealed the fate of the kingdoms of old Mexico."[41]

The natives who joined Cortés saw immediate benefits for themselves in getting out from under the control of the Aztecs. They did not foresee that a Spanish victory not only would take power from the Aztecs but would also change the entire native way of life.

Cortés's Ability to Take the Offensive and Keep It

Only weeks after the Spaniards' disastrous retreat from Tenochtitlán, Cortés resumed his attack on Aztec allies. This move was another example of Cortés's ability to seize the offensive. From detaining Montezuma's tax collectors to taking the emperor captive, Cortés succeeded in gaining the upper hand before situations could turn against him. Even as hard-pressed as he was at the battle of Otumba, he made a bold strike, saving his men from almost certain extinction with his unexpected attack on the Aztec leader.

Cortés's daring moves, on the battlefield and off, took the enemy by surprise. When he detained the tax collectors, both the subject Totonacs and the Aztecs were said to be astounded at this insulting treatment of Montezuma's representatives. Similarly, Montezuma was shocked when he realized that Cortés was taking him captive. It was simply unthinkable to subject the Aztec emperor, whose person was almost sacred, to imprisonment, even in a palace. Unable to even imagine that their ruler could be so affronted, the Aztecs were unable to counter Cortés's initiatives. The unpredictability of his behavior kept them off balance. In this sense, the very unusualness of the Spanish was an advantage. The Aztecs never knew what might happen next. Consequently, they often could not react effectively to Cortés's surprising moves.

Cortés's Ability to Keep His Men Together

Cortés's ability to inspire, retain, and even force the loyalty of his troops helped him keep together the band of Spanish soldiers responsible for the conquest. The men in the original group under his

In addition to the Spaniards' superior weapons, Cortés's brilliant leadership gave his army a clear advantage over the Aztecs.

command included not only those loyal to him but also men with ties to Governor Velázquez. When Cortés, by founding Villa Rica and preparing to go to Tenochtitlán, made it plain that he intended to exceed the mission the governor had authorized, some of Velázquez's men had wished to leave his service and return to Cuba. To eliminate that option, Cortés had the expedition's ships run aground. With no way to return home, the men were then able to be persuaded by Cortés's promises of gold and glory, and they followed him on his march inland.

According to soldier Bernal Díaz, Cortés was an eloquent speaker who flattered his men's courage and rallied their best efforts. Reminding them that they were fighting for the glory of God and in the service of the Spanish king, he lured them with visions of wealth. Those who were insubordinate he threatened with harsh punishments and even death.

Cortés's diplomatic skills, helped by bribes of gold, played a vital role in increasing the number of Spanish soldiers under his command, for he convinced most of the men from Narváez's expedition to follow him back to Tenochtitlán. More than eight hundred men from the expedition that had been sent to arrest Cortés instead joined his forces, switching their allegiance after the captain general had defeated Narváez. Many of these soldiers, inexperienced in fighting with natives, died in the Noche Triste, and after that disaster, many men wanted to return to the coast and wait for reinforcements before resuming the struggle. They even threatened a rebellion. In the end, Cortés talked them out of deserting him during wartime, promising to let them go back to Cuba when a chance arose. Meanwhile, he kept their crucial support as he planned his next attacks.

The Aztecs' Interrupted Leadership

In contrast to Cortés's uninterrupted leadership of the Spaniards, the Aztecs were led by three emperors during the two years of the conquest. Since the Aztec emperor occupied a position of semisacred power, supported by both religious and military authority, his selection involved many considerations. The new emperor was selected from a group of candidates, all of whom had a claim to the throne through a personal relationship to the previous emperor or one of his wives. The different interests and claims of many factions had to be reconciled in choosing the new leader. Once the emperor was selected, lengthy ceremonies were necessary to properly install him in office.

After the death of Montezuma, the Aztecs began the complicated procedure of installing their new ruler. The process took months, beginning with four days of inactivity while the ruler-to-be retired to a ritual center for a period of withdrawal that initiated the rites. The new emperor Cuitláhuac ruled for only eighty days before dying of smallpox. With his death, the process of choosing and installing a new emperor began again. These interruptions in native leadership handicapped the Aztecs' ability to make decisions and implement strategies in response to Spanish initiatives. Meanwhile, the Spaniards were at work strengthening their position in and around the Valley of Mexico as they prepared to renew the struggle for Tenochtitlán.

Cortés's Determination and Commitment

Though the Spanish numbers were relatively small, Cortés had the advantage of leading soldiers who were always ready for battle. They had no other duties, no farms to tend or families and territories to defend.

They slept in their armor, swords by their sides, and always had guards and sentries posted. They could move quickly and were relentless and undistracted in their pursuit of a very clear goal: winning the empire.

Their determination was driven by dreams of wealth and power. Their commitment was strengthened by a sense of religious mission,

 ## The Difficulties of Fighting on Causeways

On the Noche Triste, the Spaniards and the Tlaxcalans who had been with them in Tenochtitlán departed the city along the causeway to Tacuba. Hoping that their flight would be undetected, they carried their possessions and as much of Montezuma's gold and treasures as they thought they could manage. Knowing they would have to cross some channels of water, they also brought a wooden bridge, carried by forty men. But the Aztecs soon discovered them, and they attacked fiercely. Foot soldier Bernal Díaz described the difficulties of fighting on causeways lined with water on one side and houses with flat rooftops, where warriors could stand, on the other.

> We saw so many squadrons of warriors bearing down on us, and the lake so filled with canoes, that we could not defend ourselves. As happens when fortune is perverse, one calamity followed another. As it was raining, two of the horses slipped and fell into the lake. I and others of Cortés's company got safely to the other side of the bridge, but so many warriors charged that in spite of our hard fighting we were not able to make further use of the bridge. The passage and the open water were quickly filled with dead horses, Indians, baggage, and leather trunks. Fearing they would not stop short of killing us, we pushed ahead along the causeway. We met many squadrons armed with long lances, who cried out at us, saying, among other things, "What, scoundrels, are you still alive?" But with the thrusts and cuts we gave them we got through, although they wounded six of us.

> If we had agreed on some sort of plan, it was a terrible one. Cortés and the captains and soldiers on horseback who crossed first to solid ground to save themselves spurred right on down the causeway. The horses with the gold and the Tlaxcalans also got out safely. But if we had waited for each other at the bridges, the horsemen and the soldiers, we should all have been finished. The reason for this was that as we went along the causeway, charging the Mexican squadrons, there was water to one side and the flat roofs on the other, with the lake filled with canoes, so that we were able to do nothing.

The events of this night, when the Spaniards lost two-thirds of their company, convinced Cortés that he would need ships in order to retake the city.

for they fought to bring their own faith to people who worshiped idols and practiced human sacrifice. Not even the narrow escape of the Noche Triste could discourage Cortés. Nor could the cautioning of his men convince him to wait for reinforcements. Cortés refused to wait; inactivity was not in his nature. Bernal Díaz says, "He was headstrong in all that had to do with war, listening to no one because of danger when there was no rational hope of success."[42]

Hugh Thomas describes the actions of Cortés: "The word which best expresses Cortés' actions is 'audacity'; it contains a hint of imagination, impertinence, a capacity to perform the unexpected which differentiates it from mere valour."[43] Even as the Spaniards fled the city on the Noche Triste, Cortés was imagining a way to re-take Tenochtitlán. To accomplish his goal, he would add another weapon to his arsenal: European-style ships that could combat the Aztec canoes. It was a plan that combined the innovative ideas and determined persistence that served Cortés so well.

The Aztecs
Besieged

Chapter 5

A FTER THEY FLED TENOCHTITLÁN, the Spanish were no longer
seen as invincible. Many of their allies withdrew support.
Even the loyal Tlaxcalans had to be convinced to maintain
their allegiance with promises from Cortés that they would have a
major share in the spoils of victory.

Cortés Marches on Tepeaca

By early August Cortés began to attack the small towns of Tepeaca,
a province friendly to the Aztecs that lay outside the Valley of Mexico toward the southeast. The road between Tenochtitlán and Villa
Rica ran through Tepeaca, and Cortés wanted to secure his supply
route to the coast.

The Aztecs did not come to aid their allies, and the campaign,
which lasted for several weeks, was an easy one for the Spaniards.
After their victory, Cortés established the town of Segura de la Frontera in the area and built a fortress to ensure safe passage through the
mountain pass to Villa Rica. In the fall, when the Aztecs did send
troops to the southeast to try to keep the Spaniards from reentering
the valley, the would-be defenders were defeated and fled.

Crisis in the Aztec Capital

The reason for the Aztecs' limited and belated response, suggests
Ross Hassig, was that their capital was still in a state of turmoil from
the fighting of the Noche Triste and from the changes in leadership
after Montezuma's death. Although the new emperor Cuitláhuac had
been selected, he was not installed until mid-September.

By about this same time, smallpox had reached epidemic pro-
portions in central Mexico. A highly contagious and often fatal disease common in Europe, smallpox was previously unknown in Mexico, and the natives had no immunity to the disease. Brought by one
of the men in Narváez's expedition, smallpox spread quickly among
the native population but seldom struck the Spanish, since most of
the Europeans had already been exposed to it.

Smallpox caused the deaths of many Aztecs and sickened many
others. The emperor Cuitláhuac became ill with the disease just
about the time the Aztecs' war season was to begin. By early December he had died. Once again, the Aztecs were thrown into a crisis of leadership, faced with the divisive and time-consuming process
of agreeing on a new emperor and repeating the complex series of
procedures associated with his installation.

The Aztecs Stay Within the Valley of Mexico

Instead of marching to meet Cortés, the Aztecs chose to stay close to
home, forcing the Spanish to expend the time, energy, and resources
to come to them. The Aztecs' strongest allies were in the lower valley, especially around the lake. Here they could concentrate the full
force of their army on defending their home territory. The capital
could be reached by land only along causeways that were too narrow
for the Spanish to make effective use of the dreaded horses. Plus, the
lake was controlled by the Aztecs' huge fleet of canoes. Since the canoes could provide quick communication and rapid transportation
throughout the valley, the Aztecs would not be trapped in Tenochtitlán, as Cortés and his men had been. Rather, the island city would
be a fortress protecting them.

Cortés's Strategy to Retake Tenochtitlán

The fighting on the Noche Triste had demonstrated how vulnerable Spanish forces on the causeways were to attacks by canoes. Since the causeways were only about twenty-five feet wide, soldiers had been easily attacked from both sides as well as from the front and the rear. Cortés knew
the Spanish could not win the capital unless they could control the lake.

He began to lay plans to build ships. These would not be the first
European-style ships in Tenochtitlán; shipbuilder Martín López had
already built four brigantines during the Spaniards' stay in the capi-

tal. Cortés had ordered the ships built because he feared that his men and horses would be trapped in the city. The brigantines were to provide an escape, but they had been burned by the natives after Alvarado's massacre of the nobles at the festival of Toxcatl.

The earlier ships had been tested and performed beautifully on the shallow lake waters. The thirteen brigantines he ordered now,

The Brigantines

Twelve of the thirteen brigantines built by the Spanish were forty-two feet long. The other, the flagship, was forty-eight feet long. Each was about nine feet across. Judging from pictorial representations by Aztec artists, some were rigged with one sail and some with two. There was space for twelve oarsmen or paddlers, six on each side. Thus the boats could sail with the breeze or be moved by manpower alone. They were built to move quickly, handle easily, and maneuver effectively.

The boats were probably flat-bottomed so that they would not easily run aground in the shallow lake. Each boat carried a crew of twenty-five, including a captain and a pilot to watch for the possibility of grounding. The twelve men who paddled doubled as fighters when necessary. Crossbowmen and harquebusiers were on each ship.

Guns were mounted on the prows, which stood several feet above the water. At the center, the boat's deck was about four feet higher than water level, providing a platform from which soldiers could easily step to land or causeway.

Building this fleet of European-style ships was a brilliant move by Cortés. The brigantines gave the Spaniards an opportunity to wrest control of the lake from the Aztecs. Native canoes, which had not been made for fighting, seldom carried more than one or two persons and rode low in the water. With superior height, a relatively large armed crew, and mounted guns, the brigantines overpowered even large numbers of canoes.

With the brigantines, it was possible to blockade Tenochtitlán and to keep enemy canoes away from Spanish troops fighting along the causeways. The Aztecs' best defense against the ships was to try to trap them with forests of stakes set into the lake bottom. But this worked only until the Spanish learned to watch for the traps and discovered that, with enough speed, the brigantines could ram through the stakes.

In his book *Naval Power in the Conquest of Mexico*, C. Harvey Gardiner observes, "Offensively and defensively the ships were a tremendous addition to Spanish military power. Captain-general and men in the ranks alike had come to consider them *la llave de toda la guerra*—the key to the whole war."

Cortés said, would be the key to the war. The European ships, bigger and higher than the small, low Aztec canoes and armed with cannons, would give the Spaniards mastery of the waters around Tenochtitlán.

In the fall of 1520 Martín López and his crew of carpenters left Segura de la Frontera for Tlaxcala; the ships would be prepared there with the aid of thousands of Tlaxcalans. Native workmen cut timbers on the mountainous slopes and brought them to the worksite, where construction was carried out under López's direction.

Cortés Gains Control of Texcoco

At the end of December, while the boats were being built, Cortés and his men began a campaign around the lake. Their goal was to isolate Tenochtitlán by neutralizing or making Spanish allies of the towns ringing the lake. The most important of these towns was Texcoco, on the eastern shore across the water from the capital. Texcoco's king Cacama, one of Cortés's prisoners in Tenochtitlán, had died in the Spanish retreat on the Noche Triste. Although Texcoco's new king was loyal to the Aztecs, his brother Ixtlilxochitl, who had for years aspired to the throne, had already allied himself with Cortés.

As the Spanish approached Texcoco in early 1521, its leaders and most of its people fled in canoes to Tenochtitlán. The loss of Texcoco was a blow to the Aztecs because it was the second city of the Triple Alliance. But its gain was crucial for Cortés, who made the city his base of operations. Texcoco was ideally located for launching the brigantines, and it was near enough to Tlaxcala to make it a good assembly point for Spanish troops. Control of Texcoco also brought under Spanish control the smaller towns to the south that relied on Texcoco for leadership. Within weeks, Cortés's firm ally Ixtlilxochitl became king of Texcoco.

Campaign on the Southern and Western Shores

In February 1521 Cortés began to move south along the lake, accompanied by half his men and three or four thousand Tlaxcalan allies. The Aztecs attacked by canoe as the Spanish forces drew near Ixtapalapa, a low-lying city at the tip of a peninsula reaching into the lake. Pursuing them into the city, the Spanish fought all day before noticing that the Aztecs had opened a dyke, allowing water to flood across the peninsula in the path of their retreat.

Cortés ordered a fleet of European-style ships to take on native warriors, who fought from small, low canoes such as this one.

Cortés himself notes that the water was already very high when he discovered it. "So I left the city as swiftly as possible with all my men, although it was now quite dark," he reports to the king. "When I reached the water, which must have been at about nine o'clock, it was so deep and it flowed with such force that we had to leap across it; some of our Indian allies were drowned, and we lost all the spoil we had taken in the city."[44]

The Aztec plan to entrap their enemies had failed. They continued to chase and harass the Spaniards as they returned to Texcoco but did not attempt a full-scale assault as Cortés proceeded to his final destination, the western region around Tacuba, the smallest of the Triple Alliance cities. The conquistadors fought a number of battles with pro-Aztec forces in the area, over a period of two weeks, before retreating again to their base at Texcoco.

Though they had met some resistance and even lost some soldiers, the Spanish had not been seriously opposed by the Aztecs as they circled the lake. And their victories had caused more and more towns to make peace with them. By the end of April, Cortés had achieved his objective of isolating most of the pro-Aztec forces in Tenochtitlán.

Cuauhtémoc Becomes the New Aztec Emperor

The new emperor Cuauhtémoc had been installed in February 1521, more than two months after the death of Cuitláhuac. The new Aztec leader was a young man, brave and bitterly opposed to the Spanish. Even while Montezuma was still alive, Cuauhtémoc had helped in early attempts to organize resistance among Aztec allies and expel the Spanish. Now as emperor he tried, as Cuitláhuac had before him, to get help from other native kings. But none was forthcoming. As Hugh Thomas says, "Cuauhtémoc came to realise that the old sway of the Mexica had depended on fear. But that fear was dying."[45]

Cuauhtémoc, the last Aztec emperor, bravely fought the Spaniards but was unable to recruit the help he needed from other native leaders.

Cuauhtémoc: The Last Aztec Emperor

Cuauhtémoc had been the king of Tlatelolco before he was named emperor. Tlatelolco was an old and important market town that had existed independently on the island but was absorbed by the growing capital city. Though dominated by Tenochtitlán, it had retained its own monarchy.

Only in his midtwenties, Cuauhtémoc was already a successful warrior. He had spoken out against accepting the Spaniards when they first arrived, and it is said that he killed a number of other nobles who wanted to make peace with the Spaniards. Under Cuauhtémoc's leadership, the Aztecs fought bravely and even achieved a notable victory, capturing and sacrificing many Spaniards.

As the Aztecs weakened throughout the siege, Cortés made several offers of peace. But Cuauhtémoc refused even to meet with him, preferring to die rather than give up. When the Spaniards finally pushed the last Aztec resisters into the water at Tlatelolco, Cuauhtémoc was apprehended in a canoe, probably trying to escape so that he could continue the fight from another base. Captured, he had no choice but to surrender.

Though Cortés had promised he would not be mistreated, Cuauhtémoc was later tortured by the Spanish in an effort to discover where the gold and treasures of the empire were. The torture apparently left him crippled. Cuauhtemoc remained a prisoner for four years until, in 1525, Cortés hanged him on suspicion of rebellion.

Under Cuauhtémoc's leadership, the Mexica and their allies waited in Tenochtitlán. Depending on who gained control of the lake, Tenochtitlán would be a fortress or a trap. The Aztecs made several unsuccessful attempts to destroy the Spaniards' partially built ships, but the construction site in Tlaxcalan territory was heavily guarded. The people of Tenochtitlán had reason to fear the ships because they had seen brigantines earlier, when Cortés had taken Montezuma for pleasure rides. On those occasions, Cortés had fired the ships' cannons and demonstrated the speed and agility of the European crafts. To counter the thirteen brigantines, the Aztecs would rely on their fleet of thousands of canoes.

Cortés Positions His Forces

By the time Cortés launched his attack on Tenochtitlán, his forces numbered about nine hundred Europeans. During the fall of 1520 and spring of 1521, men from several Spanish expeditions had moved inland to join Cortés. And his supplies had been augmented with more of the important horses, firearms, and gunpowder.

Cortés reports, "I called all my men out on parade and reckoned eighty-six horsemen, 118 crossbowmen and harquebusiers, some seven hundred foot soldiers with swords and bucklers, three large iron guns, fifteen small bronze field guns and ten hundredweight of powder."[46]

He divided the men into two large groups, one to fight on the water and one on land. Three hundred men, in units of twenty-five each, were assigned to twelve brigantines. Each unit included crossbowmen and harquebusiers. Cortés himself was on the flagship, a larger boat that commanded the rest.

The land forces were divided into three groups, each with about 150 foot soldiers, 30 horsemen, and 18 crossbowmen or harquebusiers. They were stationed at Tacuba, Coyoacán, and Ixtapalapa, the three mainland towns that controlled access to causeways. These three units were to fight their way into Tenochtitlán.

The Spanish were aided by a large number of Tlaxcalan troops. Estimates vary between ten thousand and fifty thousand men. Other natives, including units led by Ixtlilxochitl, the new king of Texcoco, also helped the Spanish cause. The defection of Ixtlilxochitl was especially damaging to the Aztecs, for Texcoco had always been their main ally.

Launching the Brigantines

When it was time to launch the brigantines, thousands of Tlaxcalans, escorted by Spanish soldiers, carried the decks and other parts of the boats (which had been constructed in sections) overland to Texcoco for assembly. There the vessels were fitted with sails and other equipment brought from ships on the coast, including the ships of Cortés's own expedition. To reach the lake, a mile from the assembly site, eight thousand native workmen labored for fifty days to dig a canal twelve feet wide and twelve feet deep.

On April 28, 1521, the brigantines were launched into the canal. Their successful completion and the digging of the canal were feats of engineering and logistics that would have been impossible for the Spaniards without the aid of their native allies.

Cortés Besieges Tenochtitlán

On May 22 Cortés began to send his land forces to their posts at the
mainland entrances to Tenochtitlán. Then he set out with the fleet of
brigantines. The Spanish fleet achieved a great victory almost immediately by capturing an Aztec lookout position on a rocky island in
the southeastern part of the lake. When a fleet of Aztec canoes arrived, the Spanish drove them back to Tenochtitlán, aided by their
ships' guns and the superior height, speed, and ramming power of the
brigantines.

To effect the blockade, the brigantines cruised day and night to
keep the Aztec canoes from bringing supplies into the city. Imports of
food stopped. The supply of drinking water was cut off when the Spanish destroyed the aqueduct near Tacuba that brought fresh water into
the city. (The water of the lake itself was salty.) These deprivations immediately began to create hardships not only for the warriors defending the city but for all the men, women, and children living in it.

The Aztec canoes fought relentlessly against the brigantines. The
natives laid traps by driving stakes into the water to impale or snag
the large boats. And they tried to lure the ships into ambushes, where
many canoes hid among the reeds, waiting to attack. They also destroyed some brigantines and killed their captains. But at the end of
the conquest, at least eight of the thirteen ships survived.

How the Battles Were Fought

After six days of fighting, Cortés closed the small northern causeway
to the mainland when it was discovered that the Aztecs were using it
to bring supplies in and out of the city. It is unclear whether the
Spaniards had intentionally left this causeway open in the hopes that
the Aztecs would flee the city that way. Cortés reports only the end
result: "Although I desired them to leave more than they did themselves, for we could take greater advantage of them on the mainland
than in that huge fortress on the water, I thought it wise to surround
them on all sides so that they might avail themselves of nothing on
the mainland."[47]

With the city completely blockaded, the Spanish continued to
fight their way along the causeways. They were aided by the protec-
tion of their ships, positioned on one or both sides of the causeway

to keep away canoes full of warriors. The brigantines could also land fighting men anywhere in the city and bring firearms and cannon close enough to be effective. They could even serve as a temporary bridge for soldiers and horses to use to cross over canals or cuts the Aztecs had made in the causeway.

Making cuts in the causeways was one of the Aztecs' chief defenses. Many Spaniards had fallen into these openings, become trapped, and drowned during the Noche Triste. In the siege of Tenochtitlán, Cortés instructed his men not to cross a cut until they had filled it in to provide a path of retreat for themselves. Whenever possible, the Aztecs reopened cuts, often making them wider and deeper, to slow the Spanish advance, forcing the conquistadors to retake the same territory they had won the previous day.

Another technique the Aztecs used were barricades, both on causeways and in plazas and other large areas inside the city. Barricades were especially effective against horses since they broke up large open spaces, limiting the horses' movements. The horses continued to be one of the Spaniards' strongest weapons against the Aztecs despite breaches and barriers designed to keep them from passing. The Aztecs tried new methods against the animals, mounting swords (sometimes captured Spanish steel swords) on long lances to try to reach the horses before they could get close.

One of the natives' most effective techniques was to attack from the flat rooftops and throw missiles down on the Spaniards. The numerous roofs allowed them to make good use of their superior numbers. As the Spanish advanced into the city, they began to destroy houses as they passed so that the natives could not use the rooftops. Much of the demolition of houses was done by the native allies who accompanied Cortés; in the later stages of the siege, native farmers were brought in for the work of tearing down buildings and filling in canals. Native allies also aided with their canoes, pushing into smaller channels and canals within the city that the brigantines were too large to enter.

Battle from the Aztec Point of View

The Aztecs were forced to divide their forces, having to defend the causeways and to maintain a guard at the palace in case enemy canoes reached it by water. Hugh Thomas says that "Women were ordered to take up the swords of their husbands when they died. There was something close to total mobilisation."[48] Cuauhtémoc was firm in his refusal to give in to the Spanish, and the Aztecs were in a last-ditch effort to save their city from the invaders.

As the Spanish forces advanced farther into the city, destroying houses and filling in canals, the residents retreated deeper into Tenochtitlán. Suffering from lack of food and good drinking water, many were dying from sickness and starvation.

Though they seldom fought at night, the Aztecs launched a night attack on all three causeway camps, but this failed to push back the invaders. Then they tried attacking with all their forces against one camp, Alvarado's post at Tacuba, but this, too, was unsuccessful.

On June 30, 1521, the Aztecs did achieve one great victory and once again came close to destroying Cortés. The Aztecs lured Cortés into advancing too quickly and used their canoes to cut him and his men off from retreat. Cortés was wounded and nearly captured. He was saved by his men, but many Spaniards lost their lives in the

Spanish forces besiege Tenochtitlán, using their advanced weapons and armored horses to secure a victory.

What If Cortés Had Not Achieved the Conquest?

Cortés was not the first Spaniard to lead an expedition to Mexico, though he was the first to venture inland from the coast. Several other expeditions landed during the conquest, and their soldiers and supplies served as important reinforcements for Cortés. In fact, more Spaniards were on the way; they had left the unprosperous West Indies in search of richer lands.

Was the Aztec empire doomed to be conquered by Spaniards invading the Western Hemisphere? Had Cortés failed, would another conquistador have come along to complete the takeover? Or was it an achievement that depended on Cortés himself? In his book *Conquest,* writer Hugh Thomas addresses this question.

It may be argued that if Cortés had not carried through his conquest, someone else would have done so. That cannot be proved. The conquest of 1520–1 required Cortés' capacity and determination to win over the Indians: above all the Tlaxcalans. Had it not been for their help, as porters, as quartermasters, and in providing a sanctuary, the expedition would have foundered. Had that occurred, who is to say that the Mexica under Cuauhtémoc might not have acquired the use of Spanish weapons, and perhaps learned to use horses? Even allowing for the onslaught of smallpox, they might have maintained a determined opposition until Spain became weary of conquering.

The Aztecs had shown that they did not lack the will to resist. Though it is impossible to know, it is thought-provoking to consider what might have happened if they had not faced the gifted and determined Cortés.

fighting. The Aztecs captured more than fifty Spaniards and killed several horses. Ten captives were immediately sacrificed and their heads thrown back into the Spanish lines. But even this grisly near-disaster set back the Spanish only briefly.

The Aztecs' Last Stand

At last, at the beginning of August, the Aztecs withdrew to Tlatelolco, the great market city within Tenochtitlán, located at the northern edge of the island. Tlatelolco had a large open plaza, where the Spanish horsemen ran at will. The starving, exhausted Aztecs continued to fight for another two weeks before sending word that they were ready to surrender.

Captured by the Spaniards, Cuauhtémoc surrenders to Cortés, signifying the end of the Aztec empire.

It had been seventy-five days since the fighting began. Naval historian C. Harvey Gardiner notes the effectiveness of the blockade in achieving the Spanish victory: "Its completeness and relentlessness might well support the conclusion that the fall of Tenochtitlán was the result more of blockade and starvation than of Spanish military might and Mexican casualties in combat."[49]

Cortés described the piles of dead and the pathetic state of the surviving population, who ran from their stronghold at the last attack.

Countless numbers of men, women and children came out toward us, and in their eagerness to escape many were pushed into the water where they drowned amid that multitude of corpses; and it seemed that more than fifty thousand had perished from the salt water they had drunk, their hunger and the vile stench. So that we should not discover the plight in which they were in, they dared neither throw these bodies into the water where the brigantines might find them nor throw them beyond their boundaries where the soldiers might see them, and so in those streets where they were we came across such piles of the dead that we were forced to walk upon them.[50]

According to Spanish reports, Cuauhtémoc was captured trying to flee the city by canoe. Aztec reports say that he was on his way to surrender to Cortés when he was apprehended. However, native accounts also say that their ruler was opposed to surrender and preferred to die. Taken prisoner and brought before Cortés, Cuauhtémoc, the last Aztec emperor, surrendered on August 13, 1521.

At that moment the Aztec empire ceased to exist. Its people became vassals of the Spanish king Charles I, who, during the time Cortés was conquering Mexico, had also been named emperor Charles V of Europe's Holy Roman Empire. It was not only Aztec power that ended with the defeat of Tenochtitlán, however. The fall of the Aztec capital also paved the way for the Spanish takeover of all the indigenous civilizations of Mexico.

Chapter 6

Aftermath

IN THE DAYS IMMEDIATELY following the surrender, the Spaniards' native allies continued to kill and sacrifice many of their hated Mexica enemies. When fighting ceased, Tenochtitlán was in ruins. One of the first tasks was to bury the dead. Besides those killed in the fighting, many thousands, including women and children, had died of starvation. While recognizing that no conclusive figures are available, historian C. Harvey Gardiner notes that one source lists 117,000 dead, 50,000 of whom had starved.

The war had disrupted families and left most of Tenochtitlán uninhabitable. Surviving residents were permitted to go to other cities around the lake. However, crops had not been planted in the valley that spring and food was in short supply, causing further hardship for the survivors.

Cortés Becomes Ruler of Mexico

With Cuauhtémoc's surrender, Cortés became ruler of Mexico. He called it New Spain of the Ocean Sea, the name he had suggested in his as-yet-unanswered letters to the king of Spain. It would, in fact, take more than six months before news of the conquest reached Spain. And while the king confirmed Cortés's appointment as captain general and governor of New Spain on October 11, 1522, Cortés would not get word of it until September 13, 1523. Meanwhile, Cortés moved into a palace at Coyoacán, on the mainland end of the southern causeway leading into the ruined capital.

Cortés kept Cuauhtémoc imprisoned, along with several other Aztec leaders. However, he left most native chiefs in place to continue ruling their towns. Some of the Aztecs' top officials, including Cuauhtémoc's deputy emperor and one of Montezuma's sons, who became a Christian and was renamed Don Pedro, cooperated with the Spanish in the new government.

Cortés Sets Up *Encomiendas*

Cortés had not found the gold he had promised his soldiers. Most of the gold given by Montezuma had been lost in the retreat of the Noche Triste, and despite being tortured, Aztec officials insisted they had no more. But Cortés did reward his main captains and special friends by granting them *encomiendas*, the right to the production from large tracts of land and the labor of natives assigned to work that land. The lands granted were usually divided along the lines of earlier towns or rural areas that had been ruled by a native lord, or *tlatoani.*

Cortés reserved for himself the areas of Tenochtitlán, Texcoco, and Coyoacán. He gave extensive lands and many workers to some of Montezuma's children, including his son Don Pedro and his daughter Tecuichpo, later known as Doña Isabel, who received the city of Tacuba. Conquistador Pedro de Alvarado, who had ordered the massacre of the nobles, received the town of Xochimilco on the southern shore of the lake of that name. Martín López, who had built the brigantines, was also allocated a town, as were many other conquistadors.

Along with the king's letter appointing Cortés governor of New Spain came instructions for how the Indians were to be treated. Specifically, they forbade *encomiendas*, because abuses of the *encomienda* system had been largely responsible for the deaths of almost all the natives under Spanish rule in the West Indies. But by 1523 hundreds of *encomiendas* were already in place, and Cortés convinced the king to let them stand.

By 1524 most of the natives in central Mexico had been assigned to *encomiendas* overseen by conquistadors. The Spaniards were supposed to convert the natives to Christianity and instill allegiance to the Spanish king. The natives were to provide food and services and pay tribute to their overlords.

Although the *encomienda* owners, or *encomenderos*, did have a constructive effect on the development of New Spain's economy, the

As the new ruler of Mexico, Cortés enslaved natives under the Spanish encomienda *system.*

encomienda system reduced the natives of Mexico to near slavery. Historian Charles Gibson recounts the abuses perpetuated by the conquistadors:

> The record of the first encomienda generation, in the Valley as elsewhere, is one of generalized abuse and particular atrocities. Encomenderos used their Indians in all forms of manual labor, in building, farming, and mining, and for the supply of whatever the country yielded. They overtaxed and overworked them. They jailed them, killed them, beat them, and set dogs on them. They seized their goods, destroyed their agriculture, and took their women. They used them as beasts of burden. They took tribute from them and sold it back under compulsion at exorbitant profits. Coercion and ill-treatment were the daily practices of their overseers, calpixque [tax collectors], and labor bosses. The first en-comenderos, without known exception, understood Spanish authority as provision for unlimited personal opportunism.[51]

Spanish Settlers

Cortés encouraged settlers to import Spanish farm animals and crops for the *encomiendas*. Cattle, pigs, sheep, goats, donkeys, chickens, and, of course, more horses arrived. Fields were planted with wheat and sugar cane, and orchards were planted with olive trees. Some of the new animals and crops presented problems to the natives. Large herd animals, such as cattle and horses, kept only by Spaniards, were allowed to graze at will, often destroying the crops of the Indians. In addition, more space and labor had to be devoted to growing the Spanish wheat that settlers preferred, since the new grain did not provide as much nutritional quality as the native maize. And the cultivation of sugar, produced as a cash crop for export, brought no recompense to the natives.

Many settlers were needed to remake the conquered land into a thriving Spanish province. Some conquistadors had already fathered children by native women, often daughters of chiefs whose fathers gave them to the soldiers as a means of forming alliances with the invaders. Many settled on the lands Cortés gave them, raising families and becoming permanent landowners in the new province. Cortés also encouraged soldiers who had left wives and children back home to bring their families, too, and help settle New Spain.

Within two years of the conquest, settlers arrived from Hispaniola, Cuba, and Jamaica, where Spanish efforts to colonize were failing. This brought an ever-increasing number of Spaniards into the country, most of whom settled in and around Tenochtitlán.

Rebuilding the Capital

Almost immediately after the conquest, Cortés began to rebuild Tenochtitlán, renaming it Mexico City. He first built a harbor, with two towers, on the east side of the city to safely house the remaining brigantines. He explained to the king that with ships he could control the city and the exits and entrances to it. He went on to say, "Once this building was completed I considered that we were now secure enough to carry out my plan, which was to settle inside the city, and so I moved in with all my people, and the building sites were distributed among the settlers."[52]

The aqueduct and pipes were repaired to bring fresh water to the city once again, and the streets were cleared of debris. The streets

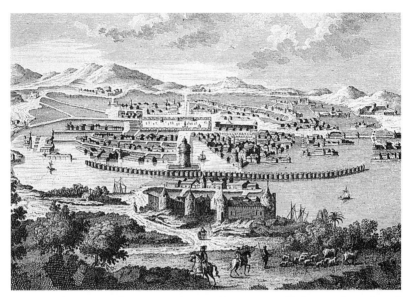

A sixteenth-century illustration depicts Mexico City, built over the ruins of Tenochtitlán.

and canals of Mexico City followed the plan of Tenochtitlán, but new streets were wider and new canals were both wider and deeper. Many canals had been filled in so that people became less dependent on canoes for moving about the city. Cortés's residence was built on the site of Montezuma's old palace in the center of town. The central city was reserved for Spanish residents, with four quarters established around it for native residents. The Aztecs would not be the important people of the new city.

Native workmen, some say as many as 400,000, rebuilt the city. They used Spanish techniques, including the use of the wheel and the pulley, along with their own traditional methods. In his letter of May 15, 1522, Cortés reported to the king: "In the four or five months that we have been rebuilding the city it is already most beautiful, and I assure Your Majesty that each day it grows more noble, so that just as before it was capital and center of all these provinces so it shall be henceforth."[53]

The city soon had 2,000 Spanish families. Within thirty years after the conquest, 150,000 Spanish settlers had come to Mexico. The culture changed to a predominantly Spanish one as the natives were required to do and make things in the way the Spanish wanted. The Aztecs' traditional crafts and material culture disappeared as natives began to use and own objects of Spanish origin, from steel knives and nails to shirts, chests, and candles.

Natives Convert to Christianity

Native religion, too, would undergo change. As historian Charles Gibson observes, "Spanish imperialism sought to justify its acts by its Christian mission."[54] In Cortés's written reports, he states repeatedly that spreading Christianity was the primary reason for his expedition.

Few Aztecs had converted during the conquest, and those who did typically did so as a sign of political alliance with the Spaniards. However, Aztec religion was restricted after the conquest when Cortés forbade the practice of human sacrifice. And, in 1525, major efforts to convert the natives to Christianity began when Franciscan friars arrived as missionaries. It was then that the old Mexican temples and idols were destroyed.

The missionaries baptized hundreds of thousands of natives into the Christian faith. Many took Christian names, but accepting the

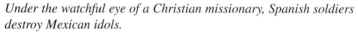

Under the watchful eye of a Christian missionary, Spanish soldiers destroy Mexican idols.

new faith was probably a superficial act for most of them. Aztec society had been polytheistic, and populations of defeated cities were routinely obliged to accept the gods of their conquerors. But the abandonment of their own gods, as Christianity demanded, was a different and unwelcome requirement. Probably many continued to practice the old religion in secret. According to Charles Gibson, the study of modern native religious life shows that many old practices have continued, some of them integrated into Christian rituals and festivals. "Although it cannot really be demonstrated, it may be assumed that the pagan components of modern Indian religions have survived in an unbroken tradition to the present day."[55]

Christian Schools

After the conquest, the old *calmecac* schools, where Aztec priests had educated young nobles of the empire, ceased to exist. But soon young upper-class Aztecs attended schools established by Catholic friars for the purpose of teaching Christian values and educating the young boys who were expected to become leaders of native society. The students learned Latin and used the Latin alphabet to write their native Nahuatl language. The old system of pictorial writing fell out of use.

The Christian monks, especially the Franciscans who came to Mexico in the early years after the conquest, treated the natives in a humanitarian manner. Many of them earned the affection and respect of the native populations to which they ministered. They were interested in native customs, primarily as a way to learn how best to teach Christian values to their new students. Realizing that the Aztecs' way of life was disappearing, some of the friars worked with native artists and elders to record Aztec history in the old pictorial style. It is from these books that the Aztec accounts of the conquest come.

Cortés Makes Further Conquests

As Spanish rule was being imposed in the capital, conquistadors continued to expand their victories throughout Mexico and into Central America. Cortés sent soldiers north into Michoacán, home of the Tarascans, who had refused to help the Aztecs against the Spaniards. He also sent expeditions east to the Yucatán peninsula and south to present-day Guatemala. Little by little, Cortés achieved his goal of bringing all of Mexico under the control of Spain. With expeditions into Central America, he extended the limits of New Spain far beyond those of the old Aztec tributary empire.

Cortés himself made journeys to the gulf coast north of Mexico City and south, beyond Guatemala, into what is today Honduras. Cuauhtémoc, still a prisoner, accompanied Cortés to Honduras and was hanged there by the Spaniard in 1525 on suspicion of plotting a rebellion. Later Cortés journeyed westward to the Pacific coast, where he once again had ships built, hoping to explore the ocean.

On his marches, Cortés was accompanied by Ixtlilxochitl, the Texcocan king whose services had been so important in the war with the Aztecs. And his main allies, the Tlaxcalans, continued to aid him in these further wars. But Cortés failed to honor the promises he had made when he appealed for their continued help after the Noche Triste. According to Ross Hassig, "Cortés had promised Tlaxcallan control over Huexotzinco, Cholollan and other cities, which had been its allies previously."[56] But these tributary cities would have given the Tlaxcalans considerable strength, and Cortés did not want to tempt his allies by handing them an advantage they might later use to threaten his control.

Native Population Drops

Within fifty years after the conquest, the native population of central Mexico began a precipitous drop. While overwork and mistreatment played their part in native deaths, by far the most common cause was disease. Smallpox, which had killed the emperor Cuitláhuac when it first appeared in the fall of 1520, recurred periodically. Other diseases, including the plague, measles, and mumps, followed. All these European sicknesses were new to the Mexicans. The diseases spread rapidly and killed many. Sometimes entire towns were depopulated, and many children were left orphaned.

Although population figures are far from certain, an effort to determine the population in 1570 estimated that approximately 325,000 natives lived in the Valley of Mexico. This is thought to be only one-fourth, or even as little as one-fifth, of the total population when Cortés arrived in 1519. The native population would continue to decline for another century before showing an increase again.

Cortés After the Conquest

For almost two years after the conquest, Cortés ruled Mexico as completely as if he had been its emperor. He settled the conquistadors on *encomiendas*, to be supported by the tribute of natives; he rebuilt the capital; and he began Spanish settlements in other parts of New Spain. He is said to have dressed in black silk, and some said he acted like a king.

But his autonomous rule ended in 1523 when four royal officials, appointed by the king, arrived to help him govern. Their appointments, in fact, were because of questions about Cortés at court. The crown was happy to accept the lands he had conquered, but court officials did not trust a man as independent as Cortés, especially when there were so many complaints about him from Diego Velázquez and others. By 1526, a commission of inquiry, called a *residencia* in Spanish, had been started to investigate the affairs and actions of the captain general. To appeal his case directly to the king, Cortés went back to Spain in 1528.

The king rewarded him with the title of marquis of the Valley of Oaxaca, a region far south of the Valley of Mexico, and confirmed his appointment as captain general of Mexico. But the government of New Spain was put in the hands of a royal committee called an *audiencia*. When Cortés returned to Mexico in 1530, he found his lands and influence greatly reduced. He also was forced to defend himself from numerous legal charges brought by enemies or disappointed members of the expedition.

Cortés retired to some property outside Mexico City, where he produced sugar and grew wheat and olives. But soon he embarked on a number of expeditions to explore the Pacific Ocean, hoping to find a passage to China. When he again returned to Spain in 1540, once again to tend to the legal affairs that plagued him, he no longer found favor at court. He lived his last years in Spain a disillusioned man, and died on December 2, 1547, at the age of sixty-two.

Mexico City in 1570

By 1570, Spain had reclaimed most of the land Cortés had given in *encomienda* grants, redirecting the profits of native labor from the *encomenderos* to the crown. A requirement that natives be paid wages for their services had been implemented, but these wages were very small, and most natives lived at a subsistence level. The natives were also losing control of the lands that had remained theirs, either individually or as community holdings, after the conquest. Little by little, especially as the native population dropped, properties were taken over by Spanish authorities for a variety of uses. According to Gibson, "Very few properties, once alienated [put under Spanish control], ever reverted to Indian ownership."[57]

Other changes had occurred over this fifty-year period. The Franciscan friars who had worked so diligently to educate the Indians and help them adjust to their new Christian culture had been replaced by priests whose attitudes were often less humanitarian. Many priests became feared for the strict measures they used to compel natives to attend mass and to make contributions to the church.

Since the new government and the new religion had destroyed upper levels of traditional Aztec leadership, the natives had no strong leaders to represent them. "Victory left the Spaniards with the political and economic power to impose their culture," Ross Hassig observes, "whereas defeat left the Aztecs and the rest of Mesoamerica with little alternative but to adapt: they had lost the power to maintain their own culture at anything above the local level."[58]

With the uppermost levels of Aztec society stripped away, the people no longer had their glorious capital, their tribute-paying

Cortés lived in this house in Mexico, but much of his time was spent elsewhere, exploring new territories or making trips to Spain to defend himself against legal charges brought by his enemies.

cities, and their ranks of costumed warriors and respected priests. Most natives became members of a large, subordinate class within Spanish colonial society. Few were literate. Some learned Spanish, but most kept their native Nahuatl, so Spanish officials needed interpreters to conduct native affairs. Not until the middle of the eighteenth century would native record keepers begin to write documents in Spanish.

Pride in the Aztec Past

Although Cortés's appointment as governor of New Spain lasted for a dozen years, his authority as ruler was soon limited by royal advis-

 ## Tlaxcala After the Conquest

Among Cortés's native allies, the Tlaxcalans were the most numerous and their services the most crucial. Support among the province's leadership for joining the Spaniards had not been unanimous, but the majority were convinced when, apparently, Cortés made promises to share power and give the Tlaxcalans special privileges after victory.

No record of these negotiations has been found. Perhaps Cortés had not intended to keep the promises. In any event, when Cortés was excluded from decision making in the official government of New Spain, the Tlaxcalans had to take their petitions for privilege to the viceroy in Mexico City or directly to the king in Spain. In many cases, they were successful.

In his book *Tlaxcala in the Sixteenth Century*, Charles Gibson writes,

> Many noble Tlaxcalans could recount military service extended to the Spanish government either by themselves or their ancestors. Requests from Indians for personal favors, such as licenses to wear Spanish clothing, or to carry a sword, or to ride a horse, were usually handled by the viceregal government rather than by the crown. Thus Viceroy Mendoza in 1538 gave permission to Francisco Maxixcatzin to carry a sword, and the permission was extended to his heir, Juan Maxixcatzin, in 1555. Other Tlaxcalan nobles requested and received comparable viceregal favors.

Later, in response to petitions from Tlaxcalan leaders, Spanish officials held an inquiry to decide whether the promises the Indians insisted had been made were valid. By that time, Cortés was dead, but several conquistadors testified in favor of the Tlaxcalans. In 1585, the entire province of Tlaxcala received the right to certain privileges, including exemption from paying tribute.

Pride in Aztec heritage is symbolized on the modern Mexican flag, which depicts an image from Aztec legend.

ers sent from Spain. By 1535 the Spanish king had appointed a viceroy, or royal governor, for Mexico. Viceroys sent from Spain ruled Mexico until 1810, when the Mexicans began their drive for independence.

With freedom from Spain came a resurgence of national pride in the Aztec past. That pride is symbolized on the Mexican flag, which bears an eagle clutching a snake and standing on a cactus. That emblem depicts the sign, told of in the Aztecs' legend of origin, that led them to their new home at Tenochtitlán, the now lost heart of the Aztec empire.

Notes

Introduction: Spanish Adventurers and the Land of Montezuma

1. Quoted in Albert Idell, trans. and ed., *The Bernal Díaz Chronicles: The True Story of the Conquest of Mexico*. Garden City, NY: Doubleday, 1956, p. 139.
2. Quoted in Idell, *The Bernal Díaz Chronicles*, pp. 158–59.

Chapter 1: The Conquistadors and Their Mission

3. Quoted in Idell, *The Bernal Díaz Chronicles*, p. 36.
4. Hugh Thomas, *Conquest: Montezuma, Cortés, and the Fall of Old Mexico*. New York: Simon & Schuster, 1993, p. 133.
5. Thomas, *Conquest*, p. 135.
6. Ross Hassig, *Mexico and the Spanish Conquest*. London and New York: Longman, 1994, p. 52.
7. Thomas, *Conquest*, p. 177.
8. Thomas, *Conquest*, p. 178.
9. Inga Clendinnen, *Aztecs*. Cambridge, England: Cambridge University Press, 1991, pp. 268–69.

Chapter 2: The Aztec Empire: A Fragile Network

10. Hassig, *Mexico and the Spanish Conquest*, p. 35.
11. Ross Hassig, *Aztec Warfare*. Norman: University of Oklahoma Press, 1988, p. 21.
12. Frederic Hicks, "Alliance and Intervention in Aztec Imperial Expansion," in Elizabeth M. Brumfiel and John W. Fox, eds., *Factional Competition and Political Development in the New World*. Cambridge, England: Cambridge University Press, 1994, p. 111.
13. Hassig, *Mexico and the Spanish Conquest*, p. 77.
14. Hassig, *Aztec Warfare*, p. 22.
15. Thomas, *Conquest*, p. 207.
16. Thomas, *Conquest*, p. 207.

17. Hassig, *Mexico and the Spanish Conquest,* p. 72.
18. Quoted in Anthony Pagden, trans. and ed., *Hernán Cortés: Letters from Mexico.* New Haven, CT, and London: Yale University Press, 1986, p. 67.
19. Quoted in Pagden, *Hernán Cortés,* pp. 69–70.
20. Richard F. Townsend, *The Aztecs.* London: Thames and Hudson, 1992, p. 106.

Chapter 3: Montezuma Does Not Resist

21. Pagden, *Hernán Cortés,* p. 468.
22. Thomas, *Conquest,* p. 193.
23. Hassig, *Mexico and the Spanish Conquest,* p. 77.
24. David Carrasco, *Quetzalcoatl and the Irony of Empire.* Chicago: University of Chicago Press, 1982, p. 187.
25. Townsend, *The Aztecs,* p. 18.
26. Hassig, *Mexico and the Spanish Conquest,* pp. 44–45.
27. Hassig, *Mexico and the Spanish Conquest,* pp. 63–64.
28. Quoted in Idell, *The Bernal Díaz Chronicles,* pp. 133–34.
29. Hassig, *Mexico and the Spanish Conquest,* p. 83.
30. Hassig, *Mexico and the Spanish Conquest,* p. 86.
31. Hassig, *Mexico and the Spanish Conquest,* p. 88.
32. Thomas, *Conquest,* p. 308.
33. Hassig, *Mexico and the Spanish Conquest,* p. 90.
34. Thomas, *Conquest,* p. 333.
35. Quoted in Thomas, *Conquest,* p. 391.
36. Thomas, *Conquest,* p. 398.

Chapter 4: Weapons, Warfare, and Leadership

37. Quoted in Pagden, *Hernán Cortés,* p. 62.
38. Thomas, *Conquest,* p. 426.
39. Quoted in Pagden, *Hernán Cortés,* p. 135.
40. Nigel Davies, *The Aztec Empire: The Toltec Resurgence.* Norman: University of Oklahoma Press, 1987, p. 192.
41 Thomas, *Conquest,* p. 430.
42. Quoted in Idell, *The Bernal Díaz Chronicles,* p. 392.
43. Thomas, *Conquest,* p. 602.

Chapter 5: The Aztecs Besieged

44. Quoted in Pagden, *Hernán Cortés,* p. 175.
45. Thomas, *Conquest,* p. 453.
46. Quoted in Pagden, *Hernán Cortés,* p. 207.

47. Quoted in Pagden, *Hernán Cortés,* p. 216.
48. Thomas, *Conquest,* p. 498.
49. C. Harvey Gardiner, *Naval Power in the Conquest of Mexico.* Austin: University of Texas Press, 1956, pp. 175–76.
50. Quoted in Pagden, *Hernán Cortés,* pp. 263–64.

Chapter 6: Aftermath

51. Charles Gibson, *The Aztecs Under Spanish Rule.* Stanford, CA: Stanford University Press, 1964, p. 78.
52. Quoted in Pagden, *Hernán Cortés,* pp. 322–23.
53. Quoted in Pagden, *Hernán Cortés,* p. 270.
54. Gibson, *The Aztecs Under Spanish Rule,* p. 98
55. Gibson, *The Aztecs Under Spanish Rule,* p. 134.
56. Hassig, *Mexico and the Spanish Conquest,* p. 149.
57. Gibson, *The Aztecs Under Spanish Rule,* p. 271.
58. Hassig, *Mexico and the Spanish Conquest,* p. 147.

Chronology

1492
Columbus reaches the Bahama Islands.

1493
Spanish settlers arrive in Hispaniola.

1502
Montezuma becomes Aztec emperor.

1517
Spring: First Spanish expedition reaches the Yucatán.

1518
Spring: Grijalva expedition reaches the gulf coast of Mexico, near present-day Veracruz.

1519
April: Cortés reaches the gulf coast and establishes the town of Villa Rica de la Vera Cruz, forty miles north of present-day Veracruz.

June: Cortés begins march inland.

September: Cortés enters Tlaxcala.

October: Cortés massacres men of Cholula.

November 8: Cortés enters Tenochtitlán and has first meeting with Montezuma.

November 14: Cortés takes Montezuma prisoner.

1520
May: Cortés leaves Tenochtitlán to meet Narváez; Alvarado massacres Aztec nobles.

June 24: Cortés returns to Tenochtitlán with reinforcements from Narváez's camp.

June 29: Montezuma dies.

June 30: The Spanish flee Tenochtitlán (Noche Triste).

ca. July 6: Battle of Otumba.

August: Cortés marches against Tepeaca and founds the fort at Segura de la Frontera.

September 16: Cuitláhuac installed as Aztec emperor.

December: Cuitláhuac dies of smallpox; Cortés enters Texcoco.

1521

February: Cuauhtémoc installed as Aztec emperor.

February 3–April 28: Cortés fights battles around the lake shore in preparation for siege.

April 28: Cortés launches brigantines.

May 22: Spanish troops set out for Tenochtitlán.

June 1: Fighting begins at Tenochtitlán.

June 30: Cortés is wounded, and more than fifty Spaniards are captured and sacrificed.

August 1: The Spaniards reach the market in Tlatelolco to attack the last of the Aztecs.

August 13: Cuauhtémoc is captured and surrenders.

1522

January: Cortés begins to rebuild Tenochtitlán.

October 11: King Charles names Cortés governor of New Spain.

1523

September 13: Cortés receives word that he has been named governor of New Spain.

1525

Cortés hangs Cuauhtémoc on suspicion of rebellion.

1535

First viceroy appointed for New Spain.

1547

December 2: Cortés dies in Spain.

1810

End of Spanish colonial period in Mexico.

Glossary

atlatl: A device for throwing darts or spears.

audiencia: Spanish word referring to a court or governing body under the viceroy.

Aztec: A general term for the people of the Valley of Mexico at the time of the Spanish conquest.

Aztlan: The mythical island home of the Aztecs before they migrated to the Valley of Mexico.

brigantine: A small, fast ship, usually with a square sail.

buckler: A small shield.

calmecac **school:** An Aztec school for the upper class run by Aztec priests.

calpixque: Aztec term for tax or tribute collectors.

calpolli: Aztec term for neighborhood or district.

Castilians: People of Castile, Spain; another term for Spanish conquistadors.

chalchiuis: Small semiprecious stones, prized by the Aztecs.

conquistador: Spanish word for conqueror; applied especially to the Spaniards who participated in the conquest of Mexico.

crossbow: A weapon with a short bow mounted crosswise near the end of a wooden stock, usually having a mechanical device to draw back the string, giving it more force than an ordinary bow.

cúes: term used by Spanish soldiers of the conquest to refer to Aztec temples.

encomendero: One who owns an *encomienda.*

encomienda: A grant of the right to the produce of land and to the labor and tribute of natives assigned to that land.

flower wars: Ceremonial or ritual encounters with an enemy using limited numbers of participants; different from a war of conquest but designed to weaken the enemy.

harquebus: An early firearm, similar to the later musket but smaller.

harquebusier: A soldier armed with a harquebus.

longbow: An English wooden bow, six feet long, that delivers a shot with more force than the crossbow.

Malinche: Aztec name for Cortés's interpreter, whom the Spanish called Marina.

Mayan: A native of the Yucatán peninsula.

Mexica: The people who founded Tenochtitlán and the Aztec empire.

Nahuatl: The language spoken by most people in the Valley of Mexico at the time of the Spanish conquest.

Noche Triste: Spanish term meaning "sad night," that refers to June 30, 1520, the night when the Spanish fled Tenochtitlán.

obsidian: Sharp black glass of volcanic origin.

pochteca: Aztec long-distance merchants.

polygynous: A form of marriage in which men have two or more wives at the same time.

quetzal bird: A large Central American bird prized by the Aztecs for its brilliant green and crimson feathers, some two feet long.

requerimiento: A Spanish legal document that the conquistadors read to the natives as they claimed them and their lands as vassals of the Spanish king.

residencia: Spanish word referring to a court or trial held at the end of a person's term in office.

telpochcalli **school:** An Aztec school for commoners.

teotl: Aztec word meaning god or demon.

teule: Spanish translation of Aztec *teotl,* meaning god or demon.

tlatoani: Aztec word meaning leader or king.

tributary: One who pays something of value to another as a sign of submission.

Triple Alliance: The three cities of Tenochtitlán, Texcoco, and Tacuba (also called Tlacopan) that made up the central power of the Aztec empire.

For Further Reading

Barbara Braun, *A Weekend with Diego Rivera*. New York: Rizzoli International, 1994. This book about Mexico's great painter shows the importance of Indian heritage in modern Mexico.

Bernal Díaz del Castillo, *Cortez and the Conquest of Mexico by the Spaniards in 1521*. Abridged and edited by B. G. Herzog. Hamden, CT: Linnet Books, 1988. The conquistador's eyewitness narrative is presented in an abridged version, with illustrations by sixteenth-century Indian artists.

Harold Faber, *The Discoverers of America*. New York: Charles Scribner's Sons, 1992. This overview of New World discoveries puts the Spanish conquest of the Aztecs in a broader historical context.

Patricia de Fuentes, ed. and trans., *The Conquistadors: First Person Accounts of the Conquest of Mexico*. Norman: University of Oklahoma Press, 1993. This selection of writings from seven participants in the conquest, including Cortés, gives the reader a sense of events from several personal points of view.

Peter Ryan, *Explorers and Mapmakers*. New York: E. P. Dutton, 1990. This general treatment of maps and world explorations includes the European discovery of America and a brief mention of the Aztecs.

Gene S. Stuart, *The Mighty Aztecs*. Washington, DC: National Geographic Society, 1981. This lavishly illustrated overview of the Aztecs discusses the people, the Spanish conquest, and the survival of Aztec culture and monuments in modern times.

Works Consulted

Matthew J. Bruccoli, *Reconquest of Mexico: An Amiable Journey in Pursuit of Cortés*. New York: Vanguard Press, 1974. This account of a modern traveler who retraced, on foot, the route of the conquistadors gives a good idea of the terrain from the coast to Mexico City.

David Carrasco, *Quetzalcoatl and the Irony of Empire*. Chicago: University of Chicago Press, 1982. This study uses Aztec myths and prophecies to present the case that Quetzalcoatl was the originator of kingly authority in Mesoamerican civilization and that Montezuma saw Quetzalcoatl's return as the end of his own legitimate kingship.

Inga Clendinnen, *Aztecs*. Cambridge, England: Cambridge University Press, 1991. An excellent social history based largely on the Florentine Codex.

Nigel Davies, *The Aztec Empire: The Toltec Resurgence*. Norman: University of Oklahoma Press, 1987. Overall assessment of the Aztecs' achievement with emphasis on factors that made it possible, especially their adoption of the role of successors to the previous civilization of the Toltecs.

————, *The Aztecs: A History*. New York: G. P. Putnam's Sons, 1974. A political history of the Aztec empire, emphasizing the period just before the Spanish conquest and demonstrating that the myth of the return of a bearded white Quetzalcoatl in the year of Cortés's arrival did not exist before the postconquest period.

C. Harvey Gardiner, *Naval Power in the Conquest of Mexico*. Austin: University of Texas Press, 1956. This study investigates the naval aspects of the battle for Tenochtitlán, including the building of the ships used in combat, and emphasizes the importance of the fleet in the conquest.

Charles Gibson, *The Aztecs Under Spanish Rule*. Stanford, CA: Stanford University Press, 1964. A history of the Indians of the Valley of Mexico from 1519 to 1810, including a history of tribes and towns in the valley at the time of the conquest and detailed studies of postconquest topics, including religion and labor.

————, *Tlaxcala in the Sixteenth Century*. New Haven, CT: Yale University Press, 1952. This study records how colonial practices affected the Indians of Tlaxcala and includes a chapter discussing the preconquest province, including its aid to Cortés.

Ross Hassig, *Aztec Warfare*. Norman: University of Oklahoma Press, 1988. This detailed look at the art of war among the Aztecs includes a chapter on the conquest.

————, *Mexico and the Spanish Conquest*. London and New York: Longman, 1994. This excellent brief treatment of events attempts to give both sides of the conflict as it explores the how and why of the conquest.

Frederic Hicks, "Alliance and Intervention in Aztec Imperial Expansion," in Elizabeth M. Brumfiel and John W. Fox, eds., *Factional Competition and Political Development in the New World*. Cambridge, England: Cambridge University Press, 1994. An examination of how states were brought into the Aztec empire and how their leadership was affected in the process.

Albert Idell, trans. and ed., *The Bernal Díaz Chronicles: The True Story of the Conquest of Mexico*. Garden City, NY: Doubleday, 1956. Detailed narrative of the conquest written by a soldier who accompanied Cortés.

James Lockhart, *Nahuas and Spaniards: Postconquest Central Mexican History and Philology*. Stanford, CA: Stanford University Press, 1991. A collection of essays on the history of early postconquest Mexico, including studies of everyday documents written in Nahuatl that show Spanish influence on native life.

Anthony Pagden, trans. and ed., *Hernán Cortés: Letters from Mexico*. New Haven, CT, and London: Yale University Press, 1986. Includes the text of five letters from Cortés to the Spanish king, giving a detailed narrative of his activities in the Spanish conquest of Mexico, with extensive notes by the editor.

Bernardino de Sahagún, *Florentine Codex: General History of the Things of New Spain. Book 12: The Conquest of Mexico*. Trans.

Arthur J. O. Anderson and Charles E. Dibble. Santa Fe, NM: The School of American Research and the University of Utah , 1975. An account of the conquest as told by Aztecs and recorded by the Franciscan linguist Sahagún, with drawings by native artists.

Jacques Soustelle, *Mexico.* Cleveland: World Publishing, 1967. This review of archaeological research in Mexico discusses the Aztecs in the context of the earlier civilizations of Mexico and includes many color photographs of artifacts.

Hugh Thomas, *Conquest: Montezuma, Cortés, and the Fall of Old Mexico.* New York: Simon & Schuster, 1993. Recent comprehensive history of the conquest, including information from previously unused material in Spanish archives.

Richard F. Townsend, *The Aztecs.* London: Thames and Hudson, 1992. A recent comprehensive and balanced overview of the Aztecs, including their history, religion, way of life, and defeat by the Spanish; an excellent source for a brief account of the conquest, with many fine illustrations.

Rudolf Van Zantwijk, "Factional Divisions Within the Aztec (Colhua) Royal Family," in Elizabeth M. Brumfiel and John W. Fox, eds., *Factional Competition and Political Development in the New World.* Camridge, England: Cambridge University Press, 1994. A review of conflict within the ruling family based on the aspirations of members of different lineages in a polygynous system; helpful in understanding divided loyalties at the highest level of rulership.

Index

Picture Credits

About the Author

Joan D. Barghusen is a midwestern author with a background in museum education and archaeology. She has broad interests in the people of other places and times and enjoys research and travel to learn about them. Her travels have taken her to Mexico where she saw artifacts left by the Aztecs of the empire period, the remnants of Tenochtitlán's great pyramid tower, and buildings showing the influence of the Spanish colonial period.